DIGITAL
ENGAGEMENT

DIGITAL
ENGAGEMENT

Internet Marketing That Captures Customers and Builds Intense Brand Loyalty

Leland Harden
and
Bob Heyman

AMACOM
American Management Association
New York • Atlanta • Brussels • Chicago • Mexico City • San Francisco
Shanghai • Tokyo • Toronto • Washington, D.C.

Special discounts on bulk quantities of AMACOM books are available to corporations, professional associations, and other organizations. For details, contact Special Sales Department, AMACOM, a division of American Management Association, 1601 Broadway, New York, NY 10019.
Tel.: 212-903-8316.   Fax: 212-903-8083.
E-mail: specialsls@amanet.org
Website: www.amacombooks.org/go/specialsales
To view all AMACOM titles go to: www.amacombooks.org

This publication is designed to provide accurate and authoritative information in regard to the subject matter covered. It is sold with the understanding that the publisher is not engaged in rendering legal, accounting, or other professional service. If legal advice or other expert assistance is required, the services of a competent professional person should be sought.

Library of Congress Cataloging-in-Publication Data

Harden, Leland.
   Digital engagement : internet marketing that captures customers and builds intense brand loyalty / Leland Harden and Bob Heyman.
       p.   cm.
   Includes bibliographical references and index.
   ISBN-13: 978-0-8144-1072-1
   ISBN-10: 0-8144-1072-3
   1. Internet marketing.   2. Brand loyalty.   I. Heyman, Bob, 1948–
II. Title.
   HF5415.1265.H3663   2009
   658.8'72—dc22
                                                2008030020

Printing number

10   9   8   7   6   5   4   3   2   1

To my wonderful family: Elise, Verity, and Nathanael.
—*Leland Harden*

AND

For Dave Smith, the smartest bear in the forest.
—*Bob Heyman*

CONTENTS

FOREWORD

BOY, I WISH I'D HAD THIS BOOK about 10 years ago, when Internet marketing was in its earliest days.

In my presentations I often quote Bob Liodice, CEO of the Association of National Advertisers (ANA). My favorite quote from Bob, though he insists he got it from elsewhere, is this: "The amount of change in marketing over the past three to five years probably equals the amount of change over the past 30 years."

How true that is! Of course much of the change we're experiencing is directly attributable to the Internet, which is upending every aspect of marketing, from the most basic strategies and tactics to even our most cherished consumer behavior models and measurement practices.

How bad is it? I make my living running a market research firm that is 100 percent fixated on covering all aspects of the online marketing universe. I'm up on all the latest digital trends; yet despite this, I still feel overwhelmed, behind the ball and, on a bad day, out of the loop. Just when I thought I'd mastered banners and blogs, or search and social networks, along came widgets, podcasts and a host of other buzzy-sounding Web 2.0 concepts. I can only imagine what it's like for the typical marketer or agency executive trying to stay current—while doing their day job.

That's why this book, *Digital Engagement,* is so desperately needed today by the management community. It is a critical, user-friendly handbook for everyone who needs to know everything about online marketing—and how to be successful at it. Beyond being a practical how-to manual, this book offers fresh insight for how to look at your business, market your products, measure your results and, most important, connect and engage your customers.

In this book, authors Bob Heyman and Leland Harden patiently (and without the usual academic attitude!) walk you through the entire land mine/gold mine of digital opportunities, each chapter starting with the strategic imperative and ending with tactical details, so you will not only learn what to do, but why you must do it. You will appreciate the further tactical assistance provided by descriptions of key vendors in the space. Plus, the book is nicely sprinkled with colorful analogies, wise insights from web industry leaders and research data to bolster key points.

Whether you're a seasoned online marketing vet or an up-and-comer in the digital boot camp brigade, read this book and share it with your team at work. You'll all benefit from its online marketing wisdom.

—Geoffrey Ramsey, CEO of eMarketer, Inc.

Acknowledgments

THE AUTHORS WISH TO THANK our colleagues who inspired us and added their insights to this book. In particular, Leland would like to express his appreciation to his associates at Hardin-Simmons University: Mike Monhollon, Dr. Charles Walts and Dr. Edward Sim from the Kelley College of Business; Amanda Etter, Kimberly Hawkins, Melynda "MO" Olivares, Brenda Harris, David Coffield, Scott Burkhalter, Robert Erin Leeper and Carlos Macias from the awesome university communications team; Dr. Shane Davidson, Dr. Bill Ellis, Harold Preston, Dr. W. Craig Turner and Dr. Michael Whitehorn from the administrative team; Russell Leavenworth, Cheryl Purcell, Mendy Huddleston, Barry Holland, Dennis Harp and Mike Hammack from the development team; and most of all Andrea Cross, his administrative assistant, for their support and encouragement during the writing of this book.

Bob sends his thanks to the team at Mediasmith for providing insight, support and everyday examples of best practices at work; and to everyone who has helped so much with the global experiment that is Kidzter.com: Jason Whitley, Dasith de Silva, Andrei Patriciu, Chad Arrowsmith, Mike Haverstock, Tardon Feathered, Lee Armstrong, Brooke Colquhoun, Robin Eber, ShariLynn Campbell and the folks at Ybrant Technologies.

We also thank those who generously contributed their data and informed us through their living digital engagement: Geoff Ramsey of eMarketer, Edward Lamoureaux from West Glen Communications, Marc Newman from MultiVu, Bruce Ertmann from Toyota Motor Corporation USA, Heather Oldani from McDonald's Corporation, Mike

Kaltschnee from Hacking Netflix, Tom Davis from Tommy Hilfiger USA, Andy Sernovitz, former CEO of Word of Mouth Marketing Association, and Mike Wilson from There.com, and our friends at Tube-Mogul, Yahoo! and Google.

Our sincere thanks also to our editorial team: Ellen Kadin at AMACOM; Mia Amato, the best content wrangler in the business; and Debbie Posner, fearless copyeditor.

PART I

FUNDAMENTALS
OF SUCCESS
FOR DIGITAL
ENGAGEMENT

GOALS AND EXPECTATIONS

INTERNET MARKETING is red-hot, once again. Television, radio, newspapers, magazines, major advertising agencies and major advertisers who once fought the tide are being forced now to redefine how they reach consumers and remain relevant. Web companies again are being bought for astronomical sums (Facebook handily rejected a $1 billion offer, Yahoo! rebuffed a $44 billion takeover bid by Microsoft and the CBS television network grabbed CNET's roster of influential tech sites for $1.8 billion, all during 2008). Some of the biggest names in web branding—AOL for one—are roiling with change.

If your enterprise sat out the last Internet revolution, got burned or came late to the party that is Web 2.0, this book is for you.

Web 2.0 brought us social networking, wikis, virtual worlds where people shop for body parts, text message advertising, mobile video search, blog pundits who can make or break your reputation and your business. This book will show you how to employ these technologies profitably while keeping sight of your goals and using best practices to engage your consumers and your customers.

These are practices that have worked for us, and for companies such as Toyota Motor Sales USA, McDonald's Corp., National Geographic, Whirlpool Corp., Dr. Pepper, Unilever and others.

WHAT DOES "DIGITAL ENGAGEMENT" REALLY MEAN?

Managing digital engagement is all about managing the participatory power of millions of Internet users to profit your business. We don't mean simply transferring portions of your ad dollars or marketing budgets to the web. Most of you are already doing that. Most of you may be quite adept at juggling marketing resources to take advantage of online opportunities to grow your business—and we can help you do this more successfully, and with more confidence and insight.

But engaging your customer within the online world requires a twist to the entire corporate mindset. It requires moving not just your media outreach but your entire organization's mission into a participatory global economy that has no borders. Imagine:

- Letting your business customers design your next product—*and* fund the product's advertising campaign.
- Becoming a household name—globally—through the power of viral online video, music and text.

This is your guidebook beyond the theoretical nuts and bolts, to tangible creative executive strategies you can use right now, with real-world examples.

ONLINE MEDIA ADVERTISING: YOU ARE SO THERE

American marketers spent $21.4 billion on Internet advertising in 2007, according to eMarketer's report, *U.S. Advertising Spending,* which also projects spending as high as $42 billion by 2011. According to this research group, the amount of online ad spending per Internet user will, in 2008, reach $100 per person if not more.

The trend for major advertisers is to pull money away from traditional media (TV, radio, magazines, newspapers) to spend more online. The top 100 American advertisers ranked by Advertising Age actually spent $230 million less on traditional media in 2006 compared to 2005, and increased Internet spending by $558 million in the same period.

Paid search (see Chapter 4) will account for about 40 percent of current online ad spending through 2011, while online display banner ads will account for about 20 percent. Classified ads, including those on newspaper websites, will continue to be explored as will social networking sites. Ad spending in social networks ran about $900 million in 2007, and about 8 percent of that went to niche sites targeted to older consumers, signaling a maturing of a market launched successfully to youthful demographics.

The numbers are important because major advertisers have signaled they anticipate a downturn in the U.S. economy, and in this report it was found that total media spending among these advertisers would increase only 2.1 percent. This means that all aggressive marketing in the next few years will be in the online space. If you are not there, you may be assured that your competitors will be.

In the key automotive advertising space particularly, a similar study by *Advertising Age* (Dec. 17, 2007) found that automakers planned for flat spending in 2008, and intended to scale back both TV and newspaper advertising, while "ramping up" online spending.

Let's face it: Newspapers, magazines, and television went down in flames in 2007—all of these traditional media sectors suffered horribly. Newspapers saw print readership decline, watched their online page views increase, and somehow still failed to connect the dots and realign their advertising revenue models. The magazine industry hemorrhaged and bled through drastic staffing cuts even as they took desperate measures to shore up declining subscriptions. Last year the Audit Bureau of Circulations (ABC) found drastic losses in readership at *Time* (–17.57%) and *Playboy* (–10.04%), while newsstand sales dropped for category leaders such as *Glamour* (–13.24%), *National Enquirer* (–15.25%) and *Good Housekeeping* (–20.71%). Interestingly, the only national publication to

Figure 1-1 U.S. online advertising spending by format, 2006–2011

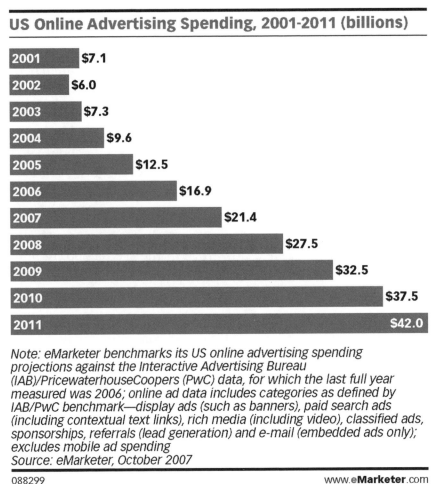

US Online Advertising Spending, 2001-2011 (billions)

2001	$7.1
2002	$6.0
2003	$7.3
2004	$9.6
2005	$12.5
2006	$16.9
2007	$21.4
2008	$27.5
2009	$32.5
2010	$37.5
2011	$42.0

Note: eMarketer benchmarks its US online advertising spending projections against the Interactive Advertising Bureau (IAB)/PricewaterhouseCoopers (PwC) data, for which the last full year measured was 2006; online ad data includes categories as defined by IAB/PwC benchmark—display ads (such as banners), paid search ads (including contextual text links), rich media (including video), classified ads, sponsorships, referrals (lead generation) and e-mail (embedded ads only); excludes mobile ad spending
Source: eMarketer, October 2007

088299   www.eMarketer.com

show a solid increase was the reincarnation of *Fast Company*, a publication that caters to Web 2.0 entrepreneurs.

The 2007 television writer's strike, which crippled American network television, had traditional advertising running for the exits and into the arms of online marketing partners. Most will not go back.

BEST PRACTICE: START WITH THE BASICS

The Web is effective for the following tasks and ROI models:

- Brand building
- Lead generation
- Online sales (e-commerce)
- Customer support
- Market research
- Word of mouth, word of web, buzz marketing
- Content services
- Web publishing

Your enterprise may require one of these ROI models, or several. Before you start spending another dime on an email campaign or a retooled website, you need to be clear as to your objectives and the expected return for your investment online. We had thought the days of throwing dollars blindly at Internet campaigns were over. But the same large companies make the same mistakes, it seems, again and again in the Web 2.0 world.

The year 2007 also saw Anheuser-Busch sink $15 million into a sponsored entertainment website whose traffic levels were so low they didn't even qualify to be measured on comScore.com, a net ratings service. Its main error may have been quite basic—overestimating the appeal of the site's main talent, ESPN sportscaster Joe Buck, as compared to the millions of available page views of unclothed females that also attract this demographic.

Wal-Mart has tried to get hip with a blog (fronted by its agency) as well as two ventures on Facebook, a popular social network site. The efforts were noted for the speed they were co-opted by consumers who used the forums to castigate Wal-Mart for some of its more controversial business practices. McDonald's, who you'd think would know something about the young people it hires, posted a recruitment page, MacCareers, on Facebook but wound up disabling the discussions after too much venting by the kids.

So let's take another look at the most appropriate web tools for each model, from a ROI perspective:

Brand Building

A recent and exciting study funded by Yahoo! showed that online web exposure doesn't just give a lift to Internet purchasing; it gives considerable lift to offline, real-world, bricks-and-mortar purchasing of consumer products. Done properly, the increase can nearly double offline purchasing.

Major marketers know this, and have been aggressively building up their websites and their web presence over the past year. A recent study by comScore, Inc. looked at the top consumer packaged goods brand sites and found that they attracted a total of 66.4 million U.S. visitors in 2007, an increase in 10 percent over the previous year. According to the study, the average customer visited a site four times, viewing about 10 web pages per visit, and spent an average of 9 minutes on the site on each visit.

Your most important tool in brand building is your organization's website. Your domain presence is both the starting point for the brand-loyal and the destination for new audiences. This is the time to beef up both domain branding (see Chapter 3) and website optimization using automated analytical tools available to all, such as Google optimizers (see Chapter 4).

Food and beverage sites dominate the consumer web space more than you'd think: In a typical comScore study of web traffic, this one covering the third quarter of 2007, KraftFoods.com was the leader, with 10.5 million visitors, followed by MyCokeRewards.com, a contest site run by Coca-Cola, with 8.6 million visitors.

Figure 1-2 Top 10 consumer packaged goods sites

Top 10 Consumer Packaged Goods Sites (Third Quarter 2007, Visitors U.S. Home/Work/University Locations)

Property	Avg. Quarterly Unique Visitors (in thousands)		
	Q3 2006	Q3 2007	Percent Change
Total Internet Audience	173,428	181,858	5%
CPG Sites	60,341	66,432	10%
KraftFoods.com	9,673	10,471	8%
MyCokeRewards.com	66	8,624	131%
Millsberry.com	4,500	4,984	11%
BettyCrocker.com	4,223	4,535	7%
Candystand.com	3,708	3,752	1%
UncleBens.com	191	3,577	187%
NabiscoWorld.com	2,394	3,325	39%
MyMMs.com	1,309	2,340	79%
Hersheys.com	1,875	2,093	12%
MMs.com	1,308	2,010	54%

Source: comScore, Inc., December 2007

Sites that sold candy or involved interactive play also were leaders, suggesting that younger web users may be developing brand loyalties online. M&Ms Candy scored well with two sites in 2007, and both of them were linked to initiatives that allow a consumer to purchase their own custom-designed colors and messages imprinted on the candies. MyCokeRewards.com is built around a contest that imbeds a code into the plastic bottle cap of each bottle of soda; a visit to the website is necessary to enter the code and earn points that can be used for prize drawings and to purchase goods.

Hershey's, by contrast, has for over a decade provided a fine example of a corporate website that manages to be all things to a broad

Figure 1-3 Pampers Denmark: forums, free samples and chat

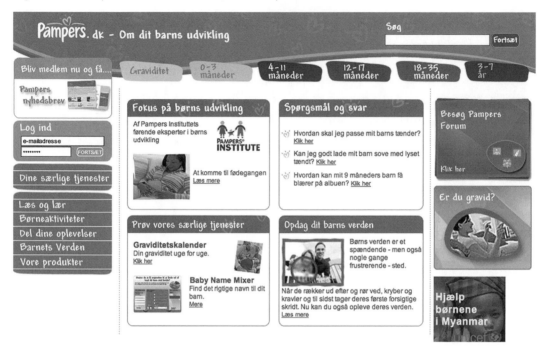

range of audiences (www.Hershey.com) that includes not just kids, but stockholders and fans of the TV shows it sponsors, such as *Project Runway*. And out of an array of hits and misses, Procter & Gamble's diaper-oriented website for Pampers (www.pampers.com) built parental loyalty so successfully it has been replicated in 48 countries and eight languages.

As a highly visited site in the consumer goods category, Pampers.com attracted 1.7 million U.S. visitors with its interactive site for parents. Not to be outdone, Johnson & Johnson recently revamped its website with video clips that show parents performing baby massage with the company's lotions.

It's fair to note that all of these and related successful packaged goods sites also pushed traffic to their websites with print advertising and web banner ads. UncleBens.com, which increased its web visibility from 191,000 visitors in 2006 to 3.6 million visitors in 2007, employed a banner ad campaign on Oprah.com and the Foodnetwork.com as well as print advertising in women's magazines such as *Better Housekeeping*.

But even these traffic levels are low compared to the *most* popular brands on the web. These are pure play—they sell things they don't own, such as Amazon.com (65 million visitors in 2007) or facilitate peer-to-peer interactions, such as Myspace.com (115 million) and Facebook (125 million), eBay.com (67 million), and gaming sites such as fulltiltpoker.com (1.5 million visitors). News sites still claim a large share of audience of interest to advertisers, and the search portals Google, Microsoft and Yahoo! are the most popular, each claiming more than 100 million unique visitors by various reporting.

But even small companies can harness the power of the web to become a household word. When Blendtec, a company that supplied powerful blenders to professional cooks, decided that its $400 blender could become a consumer product, it went way beyond any late-night television commercial. Instead, it gave itself a MySpace page and began cranking out wacky viral videos that showed how the blender could happily reduce anything to pulp—including, most famously, a similarly expensive Apple iPhone.

"Will it Blend?" put the company on the radar and the campaign made several "best of web" honors throughout the advertising community, at very little cost (beside that one pulverized iPhone). Today willitblend.com sells blenders—and T-shirts, and a DVD of its 50 most popular web videos. And it encourages web visitors to suggest "items to blend" in future escapades.

Lead Generation

This is the realm where legitimate emails face off against spam, and ad-server networks continue to get slapped on the wrist (if you consider a

$2 million fine from the Federal Trade Commission a slap) for spying on browsers and serving up unsolicited emails to the unwary who click on what they believe to be a branded contest or sweepstakes online.

Email solicitations are still what most marketers think of when they think about online. Despite its popularity, less than 2 percent of all online ad spending is spent on email. As several dozen books have been written on how to craft the perfect email pitch, we'll limit our comments to a single suggestion: test, test, test campaigns in small batches to optimize and get the most from your efforts.

Search marketing is a form of lead generation, as are banner ads. Because both of these forms of web media also perform functions of branding and awareness, their relative effectiveness is hard to pin down—and often in error. (See Chapter 10 for a further discussion of "click attribution" issues.)

New tools for both are animated or interactive applications that dynamically adjust depending on the environment for the ad, for example, a banner ad that includes a phone number that is different depending on where the banner runs. In fact, simply including a phone number in a banner ad has been shown to improve response by an average of 20 percent—which is probably equivalent to the percentage of potential customers who still feel more secure dealing with a human voice.

Affiliate marketing, where other websites provide a link to a merchant's product and receive a "referral fee" if the product is sold, is an unloved child of web marketing, and for no good reason. Amazon led the way and still boasts over a million "partners" who link to Amazon from their websites in exchange for pennies each time they deliver a paying customer to the giant online retailer. The value proposition makes sense for any marketer charged with keeping customer acquisition costs down.

The small enterprise can still benefit from linking with strategic partners that share a customer base but do not directly compete. Today, most affiliate networks are managed by service companies that recruit and monitor linking partners for you. Increasing leads through affiliates can't be hands-off, however; providing sales collateral and incentives on a regular basis to all of your best web partners can turn them into brand advocates. (For a discussion of affiliate marketing, see Chapter 7.)

If your trade is ideas rather than products, exchange of blog links through syndication and RSS feeds is an investment of time rather than money. Adding reciprocal links to a company's blog pages is a strategy that can generate sales leads if the focus remains on community relations rather than a hard sell (see Chapter 8).

Online Sales (e-Commerce)

Unlike branding, where success can sometimes be intangible, web commerce is easy to track. It's easy to see if your efforts are working or not—your products are either selling through online channels, or they are not.

While anyone with a laptop and a post office box can start selling stuff online, thoughtful online selling means delicately separating out specific channels—direct to consumer through your website, through wholesalers or retail partners, through direct email solicitation—and deciding where products can sell most efficiently. These channels must also play nice with your existing sales channels, such as mail order catalogs, brick-and-mortar retail partners, franchise operations, and perhaps a physical store that sells your products as well as your services.

It's the marketer's job to make sure that online initiatives promote product sales support and do not undermine other sales channels. If a product is less expensive online than in a store, in-store sales may suffer. If staff are compensated more for phone sales than they are for web sales, web sales will suffer. Channel conflict will sandbag your operations and should be ironed out, or at least anticipated, before you begin.

That said, consumers love to shop online. American consumers spent more than $26 billion on retail e-commerce sites during the 2007 Christmas season, a nearly 20 percent jump from the previous year. This leap, as reported by comScore, Jupiter Research, Forrester and even CNN (Dec. 26, 2007), is projected to be higher for 2008 as higher gas prices make online shopping even more attractive to consumers. Web shopping is particularly helpful for products needed quickly (holiday gifts) and those that require a large degree of personalized product selection. It's no accident that industries that have relied on personal rapport—such as travel agents, personal stockbrokers, and human resources management—have all suffered through Internet commerce. For many, it's easier to make an airline reservation or execute a stock buy online, on a 24/7 schedule.

The best movers in travel and finance recognized this early. Schwab, for one, offers its customers a choice of interactive website, phone support, and personal service through www.schwab.com. Major airlines got on the clue train after Priceline.com proved that airline customers wanted more transparency in fare options, and American Airlines, Continental, Delta, Northwest and United Airlines created Orbitz.com as a joint venture, to compete and recoup more revenue from last-minute unsold seats.

In the business-to-business space, online shopping has proved a boon for busy entrepreneurs who can order their office chairs and Post-it® notes from Staples.com, and get steel fabrication done to specifications at a competitive price through Thomasnet.com, a clearinghouse that enables industrial companies to bid on projects in the global marketplace. Need some plastic extruded next week in Peoria? A Google search on "plastic extruding service in Peoria" turns up several, with www.itascaplastics.com in St. Charles, Illinois, conveniently set up with an online RFQ engine that allows you to bid out the job immediately.

Customer Support

Everyone has an anecdote or two about their experience with a call center operator from a major bank, telecom, or software company. A faraway entity with a funny accent and a lower cost has made international outsourcing for customer service both a bane and a boon for American companies.

Domestic or abroad, customer service centers that rely on web-only interactions with customers are usually far less expensive than a phone call center. They operate 24/7, and for those customers who need a little extra handholding, usually provide "live chat" through text fields or voice-over-Internet protocols (VOIP) as well.

Smaller companies reap a much larger benefit from web-based customer support. An investment of time in a company FAQ (frequently asked questions) web page can satisfy most customer queries. Interactive "help menus" that let customers answer yes or no questions and hop through a variety of fields to solve their own problems seem to be much more satisfactory to many than going through the endless loops of "Press 1" voicemail hells.

It's no coincidence that both Amazon and eBay appear to have no telephone access to customers. Given the volume of customer queries, automated response systems are required. Nearly all web companies, however, allow queries through email, as a form field or a web address such as info@company.com.

Responsiveness, however, is key. A few years ago a survey of Fortune 100 companies found that many took two or three days to respond to an email query. Today the gold standard is 24 hours or less. Best practice often means a follow-up email to the customer, to determine if the issue was resolved to the customer's satisfaction.

The Web 2.0 version of "customer service" has been elevated to "customer engagement." We've all seen plenty of news sites and blogs that egg visitors to send in a photo of a child or a pet. A simple campaign created by WineEnthusiast.com offered a 15 percent discount to customers who sent in a cell phone photo of its weekly newspaper advertisement. By making use of a behavior well known in cell phone users—snapping pictures and then emailing them to friends, the wine lifestyle retailer not only supported a concurrent print promotion, it could then repitch the customer with mobile phone–delivered content or another offer, using an image-recognition and ad-server platform created by SnapTell.com.

Several major advertisers have solicited their consumer base to send in homemade commercials to their websites, usually as a contest entry. Frito-Lay pushed the envelope when it set up a MySpace page to launch a contest for people to create 30-second TV ads for snack food Doritos, the winner to be aired on a Super Bowl telecast. Videos of the finalists and the winners, out of several hundred entries, were probably the only TV spots to air that were not created by an agency, and they continue to be replayed on YouTube and other video sharing sites.

The only negative feedback to this successful campaign was that finalists failed to illustrate the wider demographics of the Doritos audience. So Frito-Lay went back to the well and created a different contest, this time asking for musicians to submit performance videos; the winner's music clip would also air on the Super Bowl. Comparing the MySpace pages for both promotions clearly illustrates that the second one drove deeper into an urban audience, and extended reach of the brand to a more diverse audience.

Market Research

Ed Koch, as mayor of New York City, had a catchphrase he used at every public opportunity. "How'm I doin'?" he would ask, nay, demand—while pumping your hand or peering into a television camera.

Online, it's easy to find out if you're loved or reviled. There are quite a few free websites that will count up your friends, foes and competitors for you. Linkpopularity.com, for one, gives good information on how many websites are linking to your home page and what they are. GoogleAlerts is a service, through Google, that will comb through that search engine and return you a daily report whenever someone posts something online about your company or about you personally.

Search engines themselves offer piles of data, not the least of which is the use of search query data to predict product demand. Google, for example, has reported a high correlation between the number of search queries for a feature film title before the film's actual release in theaters and its success or failure when it opens nationwide.

This opens possibilities for any product (or idea) that requires a high level of prelaunch buzz to be successful. Microsoft recently opened up its Keyword Services Platform (KSP) to developers, intending perhaps to encourage more experimentation in keyword search among potential customers of its paid-search listings service. One result has been that paid search customers can peek in better on what consumers and business customers are searching for on MSN.com, and use this information to shape products specifically for an online marketplace

Data mining your own sales data (see Chapter 10) is always recommended to discover patterns in purchasing behaviors and website usage. A number of software firms specialize in automated programs that can turn up data. Online focus groups are currently popular—you can set these up yourself, recruiting among your customer base, or use a service to round up people who will kick the tires on a proposed new product or advertising campaign slogan. The advantages of a virtual focus group are lower cost and far less time; premiums to the participants can usually be lower, there is no travel time or special rooms to set up and the inability of participants to "see" each other tends to keep the topics literally more focused, with less "small talk."

If you're pressed for time and need industrial data quickly, a flock of information aggregators will do it for you. One such is StrategyEye, a London-based company that scans the Internet, including blogs and social networks, for postings about a particular product or company. Combining search technologies with analysis, the company provides daily or weekly reports on a subscription basis, with fees running from $5,000 to $100,000. A cheerful website allows clients to access the data, add comments, supply data to the analysts, and interact and email with other clients in a common space as if it were itself a networking site. Initially designed as a "track the buzz" service for entertainment clients, the roster of clients has included IBM, MTV, AOL, Disney, Nokia and Vodafone. The website: www.strategyeye.com.

Word of Mouth, Word of Web, Buzz Marketing

Finding out who is talking about you is one thing. Getting millions of people to spread your message virally through the web is a Holy Grail of web marketing. Often called guerrilla marketing or viral marketing, generating buzz usually costs nothing but a few minutes of your time sending out a few emails to well-placed journalists on major news sites, gossip sites, user groups, news groups, blogs or an interlinked network of sites interested in your topic.

Peer-to-peer marketing came of age when it was recognized that marketing artifacts, such as banner advertisements, links to interactive web pages, audio clips and video could be passed around by emails. People did it among themselves—bypassing the originating organization entirely. Entire books have been written about how to cultivate packs of "evangelical" customers who would pass along coupons, discount codes or special notices of sales and events to their friends and relatives through email forwards.

Generating buzz got easier in the Web 2.0 world. People found friends by the hundreds on social networking sites, and with widgets, links insertions and similar pass-alongs, could spread news exponentially and often more effectively than a journalist or a web newswire release. A few million bloggers, many linked to each other and to aggregate publishing sites such as technorati.com, troll the web for "news" and are often thrilled to pass along a juicy tidbit regarding a new product or revolutionary idea. The downside to this is that juicy tidbits can be tossed to the ravenous blogging hordes from unhappy customers, business rivals, or disgruntled employees, too.

It is not always possible to control word of mouth, but it should always be within one's media tool kit, and used when necessary (see Chapters 5 and 8).

Content Services and Web Publishing

Content is king. Even if you're selling a nuts-and-bolts product, or don't have the remotest idea of how to migrate your company's mission onto the web, try this: write a book.

Seriously, according to Nielsen Online, a survey of 26,312 people in 48 countries found that 41 percent of Internet users had bought books online. In the United States, about 38 percent of online users bought books—translating to about 57 million book buyers. The greatest increases, however, were for book buying in South Korea (58 percent) and India (46 percent).

Book publishing sites such as www.lulu.com make it easy to publish electronic and print-on-demand books that look professional and can be included on the vast e-commerce engine that is Amazon.com. While

Percentage of Internet Users Who Buy Books Online

1. South Korea—58%
2. Germany—55%
3. Austria—54%
4. Vietnam—54%
5. Brazil—51%
6. Egypt—49%
7. China—48%
8. India—46%
9. Taiwan—45%
10. UK—45%

Projection and Source: Nielsen Online

you may not make millions self-publishing a book, it's another way to extend your organization's brand into cyberspace.

Content Kings: Winners and Losers. What's so funny is that companies you think would be highly successful online—major book publishers, newspaper owners, music companies, movie studios—are generally the worst flops in the content model. Newspapers, for example, have been waging a losing war against the web. Subscriber rates are down, real estate, auto and employment advertisers have been deploying more ad dollars to website listings that pull more and cost less. Music conglomerates are ready to jump off a cliff. They've suddenly realized, about eight years late, that people would rather download music digitally, a song at a time, purchasing only the songs that they like, rather than take the time and effort to buy or even rip off a compact disk containing a dozen or more tracks. And, like book publishing companies, they have discovered that overnight delivery isn't fast enough for a web generation that wants its entertainment *right now*.

Television and movie studios have fared better. Increased access to broadband allows entire feature films to be downloaded within minutes, and viewed with digital clarity in the highest definition currently available on a screen. Studios, who have always carried a grudge against the home video market, were eager to bypass last year's shootout between regular HD-DVD and Blu-Ray. They went straight to the web. In fact, Paramount, a major movie studio, distributed a comedy film entirely by web. While *Jackass 2.5* wasn't a success, it was a milk run for a process that will soon be standard procedure for all television programs and major motion pictures. Sports will likely be first. Football, baseball and basketball will become completely pay-per-view.

Newspapers have fumbled online, failing to migrate their core premise—locally relevant information—to readers on the web. Locally relevant information now lives on websites such as Craigslist, Monster.com, CareerBuilder, eBay, Hotjobs, Yahoo! and Yelp.com that serve

Paramount Not Afraid to Fool with "Jackass"

. . . On Dec. 19, the studio will make "Jackass 2.5" available in connection with Blockbuster's Movielink service. The hour-plus film has original material and previously unseen outtakes from the second "Jackass" movie in 2006. The new movie, made for less than $2 million, will stream for free but will have 15- or 30-second commercials before and after it plays.

At the same time, the studio's fellow subsidiary of Viacom, MTV Networks, and the creators of the "Jackass" franchise are using the new film to attract traffic to jackassworld.com, now under construction. . . .

The production cost, executives said, is being recouped by a license-fee guarantee, in the low seven figures, that Blockbuster agreed to pay for a one-week exclusive.

On Dec. 26, the movie will be available on download-to-own retail sites like iTunes and Amazon.com, for $10 to $15, and a DVD—including 45 minutes of extras—will also go on sale, for $30.

Beginning Jan. 1, advertising-supported streaming sites like Joost will let viewers watch the movie, or selected bits, for free. And in February the movie will be offered through cable and satellite TV video-on-demand services.

Paramount will keep 70 percent of online sales proceeds, executives said. . . .

(*Source: The New York Times*, Dec. 13, 2007)

up highly specific—make that GPS-specific—local data along with nationally trending news.

The notable exception in newspapers has been the *Wall Street Journal,* which migrated a key element of its successful print operation onto the web as www.wsj.com. The core premise of the *WSJ* was not that it provided financial wisdom, since many other publications, and no-fee websites, could also provide stock tables and financial analysis that was as good or better.

No, the core premise of the *WSJ* was that it charged an extremely high price for an annual print subscription, compared to other newspapers, cultivating an exclusivity well suited to the well-paid suits who monitor financial markets. So it adopted a paid subscription model for the online edition as well. And, cleverly, offered packages of both so readers could hedge their bets, so to speak, and get their news from either edition.

When the *Wall Street Journal* was purchased in 2007 by Rupert Murdoch and News Corporation, it was widely floated about that the web edition would soon be free. After all, the *New York Times* had earlier that year discontinued its "Times Select"—a web-only version that was restricted to registered customers that, despite web page views in the millions, had reached only about 250,000 subscribers at its peak

We weren't surprised when News Corporation announced in early 2008 that it would, instead, raise the price of the online edition from $99 to $119, following a few weeks of introductory price discounting to $79. This protected what it offered to advertisers—an audience of financially savvy, well-heeled customers who preferred top shelf to the well. The move also bolstered its value to customers—who could continue to enjoy the feeling of smug exclusivity, and could still write off their subscriptions as a business expense at tax time.

An interesting experiment going on at the same time is to allow some online content viewable for free on Google News. *WSJ* execs say the goal is to monetize traffic from the search engine with accompanying advertising, while providing an entry point for potential new subscribers to the online edition.

Having expensive content certainly helps the revenue model. The job is harder if your competitors are giving away similar content faster, and for free. Not better, just free-er. An example of a company that has failed to migrate efficiently is Encyclopedia Britannica, which earned $650 million selling print editions back in 1989. Even with CD-ROM, bundled licensing deals, and online editions selling for about $65, the reference bellwether is reduced to selling ads on its website and scraping by with revenues that hovered at $50 million in 2007. Its piece of the online reference pie has now considerably shrunk by user-generated, free competitors such as Wikipedia and Encarta.

Clearly, the way to succeed as a content company is to supply exclusive content at a price that is agreeable to the customer. This can be a 99-cent music download or it can be a $2,000 business marketing report. Immediate delivery of content ups the value of the content proposition, and this can be done in most cases through broadband web media.

Ad-Supported Content Services and Content Publishing. If you're in the business of collecting or aggregating information, and rely upon the ad-supported model of publishing, you're playing by different rules. Your content is free to all. You strive to make it exciting enough so thousands if not millions of eyeballs flock to download it. You make your money by selling advertising space in and around the content, and your rates are based upon the number of eyeballs you attract.

Web publishers and news aggregators are enjoying a resurgence with the new boom in paid advertising—banners, animated advertisements chock full of video, music and interactivity and click-through search ads. The whole concept of the World Wide Web, where hyperlinks can be clicked and users can navigate from site to site, make it easy for any website to support and gain additional revenue through advertising. What this means, of course, is that every website that attracts your customer category can compete not just for your eyeballs, but for your advertisers as well. In business-to-business and business-to-consumer arenas, pricing formulas and audience reach can be improved by partnering with an online advertising network, such as DoubleClick or Google. This allows even the lamest content sites such as Encyclopedia Britannica to sport ads for Chevrolets and Mountain Dew.

Getting content on your website is easy—you just link up to other sites with real information, pull in a few relevant RSS feeds and become known as an aggregator. The links are free, and all you need to add is some witty or sarcastic commentary and you are well on your way to instant fame as a blogger extraordinaire, or an expert source in your field of endeavor.

Getting revenue is trickier. Eyeballs can be counted (page impressions, unique visitors, page visits, duration) as are click-throughs. As many advertisers will pay only for countable click-throughs, well-planned ad revenue strategies will survive being paid on a performance basis, and will build in routine promotions to keep traffic levels high. At its best your strategy will deliver a targeted audience and qualified leads to the advertiser, and be unique enough to draw back that audience, and new audiences, time and time again, with fresh and exciting content.

Two of the biggest success stories coming out of the television industry have been ESPN.com and CNN.com. These web operations far outstrip anything done in the television realm in terms of reach and content aggregation, and both groups remain true to their brand's core mission—delivering news or sports scores faster than their competitors. They realized early on that web audiences didn't necessarily want to watch television to get their international news and sports information. What people want is to get the information—period—and if they can get it faster and more efficiently on their office computer, PDA or mobile phone or pager, they will. Both CNN and ESPN link to other, even competing, sources if it means they can post the most comprehensive aggregate of information on their home site.

Having the backing of a giant media conglomerate is no guarantee; the parent companies of both ESPN (Disney) and CNN (TimeWarner) have crashed and burned a few sites over the years that delivered nothing more than cheer to their rivals.

RSS, CSS, web tags and related blog technologies on your website make it easy for smaller operations to aggregate and win. Thus, Smoking Gun, the Drudge Report, Deadspin.com and local sports blog sites such as www.blackshoediaries.com can and do compete for eyeballs and national and local advertising dollars.

Blackshoediaries.com, a college sports blog, sells web ads directly for $20 per week—and through the blog advertising network Federated

Media (www.federatedmedia.net [not to be confused with Federated-Media.com, which handles ad sales for the websites of a string of soft rock radio stations in Indiana]).

A newer company you may have heard of is Veoh (www.veoh.com), which aggregates video content and has managed to assemble an impressive list of content sources—and advertising clients—in a very short time. As a video sharing platform (think of it as a higher end YouTube) it got the jump on Hulu.com despite the latter being a team effort of NBC and News Corporation to produce high-definition TV online.

Not only does Veoh deliver free video downloads of favorite TV shows such as *CSI, 24, The Office, The Simpsons,* and CBS News, the site allows individuals to "publish" homemade or professionally made videos on a platform that makes them available to the entire web. It automatically syndicates the videos to YouTube, MySpace and Google Video and converts the feed so it can be played back on something as small as an iPod screen.

Many of the services on this video hosting site are free; programs themselves can be set up by their producers as free, pay-per-view or ad-supported. Organizations can also create their own "channels" on Veoh. (For more on web video advertising, see Chapter 6.)

CASE STUDY: Kidzter.com—Launching into Kid Space

Bob Heyman's www.kidzter.com site provides an example of several of the techniques and strategies discussed in this book. The content is largely via aggregation. The talent creating the site is mostly outsourced. The revenue depends upon the affiliate "freemium" business model and marketing is via search, viral video and social networks.

Kidzter is a kid's web portal hosted by the Rockabyes, an animal character rock 'n roll band. The site includes original games, a video player, a song jukebox, and a "haunted" rock 'n roll mansion (a virtual world in which kids can customize rooms).

The singing voices of the band are provided by legendary real musicians, such as Maria Muldaur as the voice of lead singer Crystal Canary and Jefferson Starship stalwart Marty Balin as the voice of guitarist Floyd Fox. Other stars contributing are Dan Hicks (of Dan Hicks and His Hot Licks), Nick Gravenites (of Electric Flag), John "Marmaduke" Dawson of New Riders of the Purple Sage and Huey Lewis.

Bob had songs and puppets that had been created. The puppets had been stashed in storage when Bob and Leland got into the Internet marketing business in the nineties. As the band, being puppets, had not aged, Bob wondered what new opportunities the Internet had brought. Surely the Rockabyes should have a website, and also MySpace and Facebook pages.

Over time, the vision expanded to the creation of a site to rival WebKinz (www.webkinz.com) or Club Penguin (www.clubpenguin.com), two hugely

Figure 1-4 Marty Balin, Dan Hicks and Maria Muldaur are the voices behind the Rockabyes

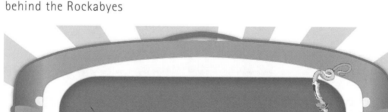

successful sites for kids. Disney had bought Club Penguin last year for an estimated $750 million, so Bob was convinced he was laboring in a potentially lucrative area, if he could create enough compelling kid's content.

But first, he needed to find an animator/cartoonist. A friend suggested advertising the gig on the Commarts.com jobsite (www.creativehotlist.com). The response was amazing. Many very talented artists responded, from all over the globe.

Bob selected Jason Whitley, who proved to be a marvel, bringing life to the characters, animating music videos and creating wonderful flash animations for the website.

Next, Bob needed a web design team to implement Jason's designs. He turned to Ybrant, a marketing services firm based in India, who could provide a low-cost ongoing solution.

While working on the design implementation, Bob needed to ensure that there was a revenue model for the site. Club Penguin charged a monthly subscription fee while WebKinz required kids to buy a toy to get the code to play the most fun games. Parents found both models wanting. Bob wanted to enable the site to be free and thus needed to find an alternative approach. He ultimately chose to utilize the affiliate model, building out shopping guides for kids and parents in the areas of books, music, video, clothes, furniture, games, toys and electronics. Bob discovered two extraordinary software programs that helped power this strategy: Build a Niche eBay Store (BANS) and Associate O Matic, which are able to suck product listings from Amazon and eBay into Kidzter.

But how to create the robust content that kids would want?

Bob was able to aggregate a large number of games without having to create new ones. And to create rich new ones on a meager budget. First he aggregated the best games he could find on other sites, collecting them on a Favorite Off-Site Games Page. Later he added similar pages for games in which kids could learn about music and sound by playing fun games and learn about ecology by playing "green" games.

Then he found that there were quite sophisticated game engines and scripts that could be customized with the Kidzter look and feel. The results include a game similar to Neo Pets, in which kids can adopt and care for baby versions of the Rockabyes characters; a "Battle of the Bands" MMORPG (Massively Multi Player Online Role Play Game); and a "Games Arcade" with thousands of Flash-based games.

In another outsourcing coup, Bob found Andrei Patriciu, a programmer in Romania who was able to help Jason build a state-of-the-art "dress-up" game, on the Rentacoder website (www.rentacoder.com), where Andrei is very highly rated. Andrei also created a Kidzter widget for use on Facebook. For webmaster and SEO services, Bob went with Ybrant. He found Mike Haverstock, a teenager in Indiana, now in charge of building Kidzter's virtual world (a haunted rock n'roll mansion) from a referral by Mitch Waite (www.whatbird.com), a tech publishing legend.

Having amassed a large number of fun games, blogs (from Typepad) and wikis (from Wikispaces) turned out to be an easy addition, requiring only tweaking the look and feel. For the video player, he chose Social Media, an Australian product. In the course of searching for someone to customize the product, Bob found out about a coder named Dasith de Silva and hired him. Only when trying to pay him did Bob find out that Dasith was a seventeen-year-old in Sri Lanka who was too young (lacking a bank account or credit card) to have a PayPal account. The amazing Dasith has since become the site administrator ("and surely will be the Bill Gates of Sri Lanka," says Bob).

In marketing and promoting Kidzter, Bob is practicing what he preaches. Besides doing organic search optimization (including workarounds for the heavy Flash site content), he has created web video assets to be distributed to YouTube and other video sharing sites. These include a few assets to attract parents—for example, a puppet-based, three-episode tribute to San Francisco rock 'n roll.

MAKING OVER YOUR WEBSITE

Can You See Me Now?

IF YOUR WEBSITE LAUNCHED more than a year ago, it's probably ripe for a makeover. Sure, you may have great plans and a budget for a terrific banner branding campaign and a killer email outreach project, but unless you tidy up at home it will all go for nothing. It would be like sending all the people you want to impress a flutter of fancy, cream-colored, heavy-stock printed invitations to a party at your house—and then greeting your guests at the door in your bathrobe or dirty underwear.

Sorry.

Tiny phone screens, other wireless mobile platforms, browser compatibility for text and visuals, global standardization, the ubiquity of broadband connections and the power of Web 2.0 applications demand that your website be not just dressed for success, but welcoming to all visitors, and that it efficiently serve and even go beyond their expectations. If your goals include maximizing click-throughs and improving your sales or brand status, all factors involving web usability should be reexamined. If you have plans for web video or viral video in your near future, heads-up: YouTube Mobile was enabled this past year for over

100 million wireless phones made by Nokia, Helio, Motorola, LG, Sony and iPhone.

Many web marketers heard the call years ago, adapting XML protocols that made it easier for a single design to be visible, nicely, on a wide variety of screens. New web designs are always evolving, and coding needs to be refreshed frequently to keep up with advances at major search engines.

A new lineup of web analytics tools make the job of optimizing websites easier. These include:

- *Google Website Optimizer* (services.google.com/websiteoptimizer): This is a free tool (in beta) available to sites with Google Adwords accounts. Extensive support, written in plain English, should make this a first stop whether or not you use Adwords.

- *Web Page Analyzer* (www.websiteoptimization.com/services/analyze/): A free version of an analysis program from Website optimization.com, a venture from Andrew King, Java developer and author. Clients have included AOL, Bank of America and Caravan Tours.

- *Web Site Maestro* (www.tonbrand.nl): Free or inexpensive shareware programs from TonBrand Products popular with Mac as well as PC fans, and especially useful for reducing image file sizes and improving page loading times.

- *Omniture Site Catalyst* (www.omniture.com/products/web_analytics/sitecatalyst): This solution allows organizations to visualize and track traffic through their site and conduct real-time tests that affect page views, entry and exit pages, drop-off and other variables.

- *Atlas Site Optimizer* (www.atlassolutions.com): Part of a suite of optimizing applications from Atlas (a Microsoft company), geared to the medium to large enterprise.

BEST PRACTICES FOR SITE OPTIMIZATION

- *Prioritize and be proactive.* Your home page and the designated landing page for any promotion should be optimized prior to any new surge in customer outreach. You test your email campaigns in A/B versions for effectiveness, don't you? Test landing pages at the same time.

- *Finalize visuals for a site relaunch some months in advance of launch,* so you can program these visuals into your marketing media one to three months prior to the relaunch. This is easier in some industries than others. Rockport, the shoe manufacturer, scheduled a site revamp for autumn, when women's fashions traditionally morph into new styles. But it launched the visuals in online and offline campaigns in early June to familiarize old customers, while rebranding to attract new ones, before the selling season began. The "stealth" relaunch—changing a look overnight—is popular with high-tech, banking and automotive companies, such as Chevrolet, Mercedes Benz, UBS, Lockheed Martin, Sony and Intel. Print, television and event marketing all launch simultaneously.

- *Design for all screens.* What looks good on your web master's 19-inch monitor has to look good on a 2-inch diagonal on a web-enabled cell phone. Make sure there is white space and clear imaging (a logo, emotive photograph or sharply defined graphics). When testing pages, borrow a variety of handhelds to view the links to your designer's mockups or drafts. Another tip: pay attention to how graphics and video clips appear as "thumbnails"—the snapshot, postage-size images are what users of cluttered social network sites and cell phone web screens see. These should render clearly and communicate on a glance what the content is about. To get ideas, take a look at mobile video gaming sites to see how sketchy, cartoony content can be stylistic, powerful and expressive within the confines of a tiny screen.

Figure 2-1 Home page content design for home computers

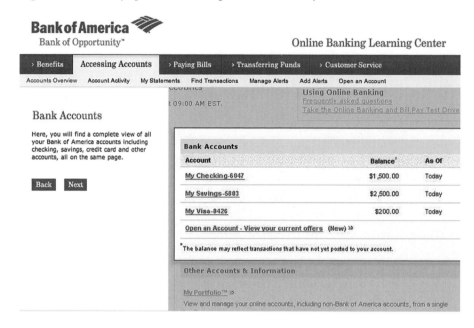

Figure 2-2 Same page content design for cell phone and PDA

- *Dynamic interface options* for your website are worth the extra effort to extend your reach and your page impression count. Some sites let customers pick from two versions: Flash or non-Flash compatible, for example. Intelligent software sniffer programs will automatically detect each user's operating system and browser and serve up a duplicate web page that contains key elements tailored to each browser, including old-fashioned "text-only."

- *Make use of visual short cuts* that savvy web users always rely on for information. Two common visuals are the blue line under text that indicates a text link, and edged rectangles that telegraph "click me here."

- *Embed trustworthiness.* Important cues are the Verisign and eTrust logos that signal that your merchant site is secure. Tasked with the job of revamping Audible.com's website, Jonathan Mendez found that making the two logos more prominent on the landing page increased both sales units and revenues by about 30 percent. If you've got this endorsement, get it up front on the landing page.

Says Mendez: "Brand, trust and security icons as well as testimonials deliver confidence messages that can have a tremendous impact on conversion. Despite the fact that we are about ten years into the commercial web, users on even the largest sites and brands in the world are influenced by these messages and images." The power of implied trust applies equally to nonprofits. Steve Daigeneault of Amnesty International USA has reported that adding the Verisign logo next to the "submit" button on its donation page improved conversion rates.

ARE PAGES APPEALING TO MODERN WEB AUDIENCES?

One of the ways social networks have influenced all web media is that the hard sell is disappearing and looks anachronistic. If you've just clicked through a widget or a link passed on by your friendly community, the destination web page you land on should look just as friendly and be compatible in look and feel with the prior web page.

Some ways to do this with text and image:

- Tweak the color scheme of a promotional landing page to match the color scheme of the blog or social environment. They're pink and green? Be pink and green. Or at least work it in, as a background color, text font color, or button color.

- Retire hard sell language like "Click Here!" "Buy!" "Subscribe!" and "Act Now!" Successful replacements include "Try me," "Explore," "Learn more," "Continue" and "Find."

- Cut steps to conversion on internal pages and forms to make actions simpler and faster to complete. Trimming unnecessary fields from a sign-up form (such as gender, business title, salutation, or even city and state) can improve sign-ups by as much as 20 to 30 percent.

Be clear on your goal here. Do you want to facilitate engagement, or are you soliciting marketing information at the expense of conversions? Would you rather have a short list of clients you know a lot about or a large list of fairly anonymous clients comfortable with transactions on your merchant site? Some of the most highly trafficked sites only require an email address for registration and participation—not name, rank, or serial number. What is the least amount of information required for lead generation if your follow-up pitch will be via email? One B-to-B website found that sign-ups increased 19 percent if a sign-up form did not include fields for a street mailing address.

If the destination page for a campaign is your home page, clear a space on the home page for the promotion. Don't make the visitor have to hunt down a left-side menu or a tiny box way down on the first screen page to find the content that corresponds to the campaign. This sounds obvious but it is not often the case if your web master is so in love with his or her design he or she won't give you room.

If you can't successfully negotiate room on the home page, take the extra step of creating a daughter site or splash page for the promotion, and link it to your main pages or relevant internal pages.

Keep navigation buttons consistent when you add a splash page. New visitors and old friends should always know where the back button is, and the location of their shopping cart. We're not saying you have to blindly copy all conventions. No rule says that the "about" section links have to be at the bottom of your home page. (The shopping cart doesn't always have to be in the upper right hand corner, although that is another visual short cut favored by many commerce sites.) Be yourself; be creative. But be consistent, page to page.

A few more tips from the voices of experience:

- *Let customers know in advance about a site makeover.* Consumers tend to really complain when a website changes its menu array. "Coming Soon!" or "Watch for our new look!" banners on a home page will keep down the complaints. A feedback mechanism such as a survey ("So How Do You Like Our New Look?") page or pop-up may encourage adoption of a new site design.

- *Balance search optimization and landing page optimization* with testing to achieve your ultimate goals. Cramming a page headline full of key words to maximize search hits may seem like a great idea until you realize a lengthy head may not be absorbable by your target customer. Branded sites need to have a "look and feel" that resembles your organization and makes it instantly recognizable. They still need to load quickly. If your audience reach includes large numbers of people using Firefox or—heaven help us—dial-up modems, lower your artistic expectations and optimize for the lowest common denominator.

- *Kick the ad server under the table* for a week or so and see if your page views and click-throughs improve. Executions for third-party served banners and videos may considerably slow down loading times to the annoyance of your customer base. This is more of a

problem with second- and third-tier ad servers but it will affect
page recording.

IMPROVE NAVIGATION TO IMPROVE CONVERSIONS

If a new visitor clicks to your site from a search query, don't serve them
up a pop-up video advertisement before they've had time to settle in.
Don't make them hunt for the "skip this ad" link. They came to visit
you—not your advertiser. Small enterprises that still need ad revenues
to help fund their core business should take a cue from blog and news
sites that take advertising that tends to be unobtrusive.

In a perfect world we'd also remove the cinematic opening numbers
that greet us on white-shoe professional sites, creative agency sites and

Figure 2-3 Scott Morris Productions serves up a visual menu

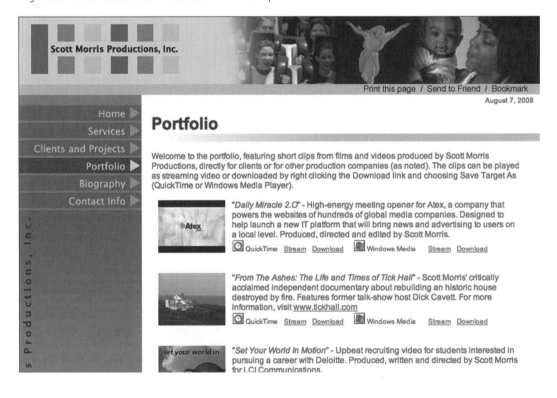

some fashion sites. If you have to include a "skip this intro" option to your intro, doesn't that tell you something? To fully engage the customer, allow them the freedom to click or mouse over a screen object to access moving images or clips. Let them make the choice.

Merchant sites that offer literally thousands of products to consumer audiences face a special problem. Site visitors typically want two things: the ability to search deeply into product categories, and constant updates on what is new, trendy and on sale.

Automating product selection solves both these problems. Improving your site's internal search engine solves the first problem. One retailer's consumer survey revealed that more than 70 percent of its customers were likely to leave a site if they could not locate a product stream within a minute or two of arrival on a landing page.

Rich-media inclusions—eye-catching seasonal or promotion-driven banners and interactive tools—help direct visitors to specific product lines while creating a participatory experience that can engage the visitor and turn a browser into a buyer. Rich-media experiences on a home page also encourage loyal customers to check back frequently to see what is exciting and new.

Future Shop, a Canadian electronics retailer, was one of several retailers to employ an animated Flash tool during the holiday sales period. A candy-striped animation served a useful purpose as a "gift guide" for shoppers who might be understandably confused by the array of wide-screen TVs, phones, computers and digital cameras the retail chain sold both online and in its brick-and-mortar stores. Selecting among several choices that described a gift recipient led visitors to a short list of products appropriate and trendy—a great shortcut to harried holiday shoppers.

The best use of rich media allows consumers to participate or not, on their own schedule. As Bob is fond of saying, "We are in the business here of leading horses to water." One example from our friends at Marketing Sherpa: MyWeddingFavors.com, an online retailer of wedding table accessories and bridesmaid gifts, tested product videos three

Figure 2–4 Future Shop's engaging gift guide

ways: no video at all, an automatic unspooling of the video when the home page loaded and a "click to play" option. Not surprisingly, allowing website visitors to view the video when they were ready improved conversion rates for the products shown in the videos by 35 percent. Allowing consumers this choice helped automate product selection, encouraged engagement through active participation and streamlined the flow of product into a shopping cart.

More fundamental changes on a merchant site may be required if your product lines or customer focus has shifted through the years. Recategorizing products may be a headache for your coding team, but well worth the lift in conversions it can provide.

Figure 2–5 Staples engages the customer with a checklist activity

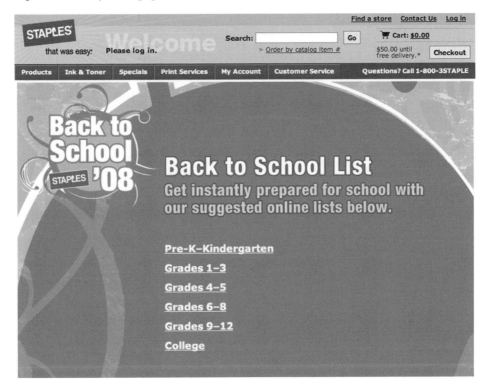

The Staples.com site offers twenty different models of photocopiers, and a roster of product-search menus that allow a customer to self-select based on function, price and brand preferences. This is a fine example of a site navigation strategy that caters to both home and business clientele.

The home page should have some dedicated space to bolster your current promotions and track their metrics. Are you presenting a special, limited-time offer only to your newsletter customers? Wait a day or two, then place the offer on your home page as well. This reinforces the offer to returning customers who opened the email, and makes it visible to customers who may *not* have opened the email. A maker of industrial products did this and saw the number of offers redeemed improve by 50 percent.

Keep the text on your home page and landing pages short, direct and, most important, fresh and focused on what's relevant to your current promotion. Keep the artwork clean and allow your visitors some visual room—that lovely white space again—to scan the page for what they are looking for. Your visitors will spend a fraction of a second looking around; if they're not comfortable, they will leave.

AUTOMATING PAGE OPTIMIZATION

Automated tools for landing page optimization began as simple HTML "editors" to clean up coding errors. Now these are rapidly maturing into on-the-fly testing dashboards that perform multivariate or A/B testing of web page design, in real time and with your real customers.

"Automating the optimization and management of your marketing campaigns leads to maximum efficiency and a minimum of mind-numbing tactical work," says Chris Raniere, founder and CEO of Revcube Media (www.revcube.com), a web analytics firm. Landing page variants aren't good enough by themselves, he says: the best testing systems are "holistic" and take into account input from banner campaigns, emails and search, as well as landing page visits.

Cutting-edge digital marketing companies such as Revcube are working to build this automated platform from the ground up.

"What does seem to work and can lead to more conversions—as well as a more satisfying role as a marketer—is integrating various online marketing programs by automatically optimizing within and across them, from engagement to conversion," says Raniere.

Revcube's technology uses proprietary algorithms and business intelligence to determine which elements are the most effective at driving online conversions. These "learnings" are then applied in real time, in order to acquire a higher volume of high-quality customers. By taking action on data rather than just reporting it, the software's automated approach helps online marketers eliminate inefficient aspects during a marketing campaign.

How to select an automation program for your enterprise? Raniere offers this advice:

- Size is important. If you are only converting a few customers per day you can be very effective in manual mode.

- Be sure at some level you connect all media placements with landing page optimization and if possible to lifetime-value data. Landing page optimization is not a stand-alone offering in the world of acquisition.

- Make sure the system does actually take action, not just spit out a report. If a system can tell you which banner is underperforming or which combination of elements on a landing page return a negative ROI, it should be able to shut them off without your input.

- Develop expected-value calculations for every placement and use them in determining daily if not hourly CPC (cost per click), CPM (click per thousand) or CPA (cost per action) rates.

"Placement to conversion should be on one platform, meaning that for every placement, such as paid search, the campaign consists of integrated decisions on keywords, text ads, landing pages and conversions," Raniere notes. "Don't separate bid management and landing page optimization. Autogenerate and optimize landing pages taking into consideration both creative and environmental attributes." He also advises: "Never take creative executions out of rotation."

CASE STUDY: **Tommy Hilfiger USA—When a Picture Is Worth a Thousand Dollars**

Tommy Hilfiger is a premium fashion lifestyle brand, covering product lines and categories organized by various divisions: Menswear, Womenswear, Childrenswear, Denim, Sport, Bodywear and other various licensed products such as fragrance, accessories and home furnishings.

The Tommy Hilfiger brand combines quintessential American style with unique details to give time-honored classics an updated look for customers who desire high-quality designer apparel at competitive prices under the following labels or collections: Tommy Hilfiger, Hilfiger Denim, and Hilfiger Sport.

Being a diverse brand with varying collections, the online challenge facing the e-commerce team at Tommy Hilfiger USA was how to best represent men's dress shirts on the web. This was not a simple task. Men's shirts represents almost 30 percent of the company's yearly top-line revenue, so it was imperative to drive not only as much revenue as possible but also to maximize profit.

Photography is a large expense for any online fashion retailer. Think about it, every time a product is added to the online store, every style, color, pattern, etc. requires a photograph.

"To add one SKU creates a cost consequence, for us," explains Tom Davis, director of e-commerce for Tommy Hilfiger USA. Further, the kind of shot must be considered. Garments can be displayed "on figure" or "on model" (with a model wearing them), "on mannequin," as "pin-ups" (pinned to poster board then mounted on the wall) and as "lay-downs" (placed on the floor and shot from above).

The team had observed that women's garments that were displayed on a live model sold better than garments that weren't, so they naturally assumed that this would carry through to men's shirts. When dealing with

Figure 2–6 Hilfiger shirts sold better without models

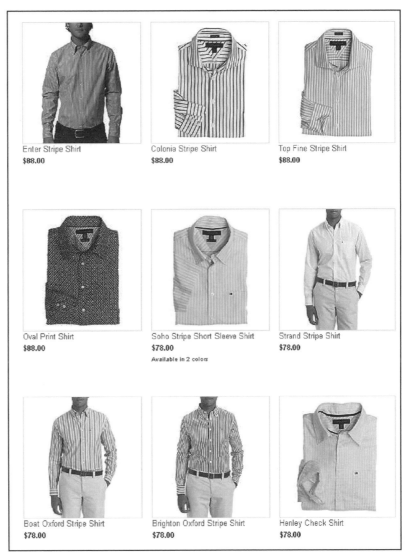

shooting striped shirts on model, however, they were having problems getting close enough to the garment to actually show the pattern and the weave, and to dissipate some of the artifacts inherent in photographing stripes. Lay-down pictures worked better for displaying garment patterns, and were less expensive to shoot. But a question remained: Could Tommy

Hilfiger cut photography costs shooting without a model and still maintain a healthy conversion rate?

The team decided to test the styling of men's shirts online. The decision was to shoot half of the men's shirts in a lay-down style and the remaining half on a model. The pricing structure to shoot a lay-down picture of a Tommy Hilfiger shirt was one third of the cost of a picture of a Tommy Hilfiger shirt photographed on a model. But the question for cost-testing was: Would customers of Tommy Hilfiger's online store show preference for men's shirts on a model?

Since customers usually shop for others during holidays, and not for themselves, the decision was made to choose a non–holiday season time of year (early spring) with a minimum of a four-week time frame as their test window. The time frame would allow enough time to even out any statistical anomalies. The marketing team was careful to promote each style of photography equally. This was performed online, in email and within the site. Email promotions each contained two shots, one on figure and one lay down. Each web page contained five of one example and four of the other. The team randomly set pictures within the men's shirt section so that lay-down pictures and on-model pictures varied. Further, the price point for each type of shirt photographed was either $78 or $88.

The results of this simple test were clear . . . and a big surprise. The less expensive lay-down style drove a higher conversion rate. Shirts presented in lay-down display sold at 3.2 times the rate of the products that were shot on a model. Further, because the cost of a lay-down photograph was one third of the cost of the on-model shot, the return on investment was recouped 60 percent faster. So, not only was the lay-down shot less expensive, it was also more profitable.

"We all thought that our shoppers preferred a model. We were completely wrong," states Davis. "Testing proved our hypothesis invalid."

The team's takeaway? Men buy based on pattern, not on fit. It is not as important to men to see how a garment fits as it is to women.

Hilfiger continues to test, and uses Google Analytics to track the traffic patterns and conversion rates on its site. "There are meatier programs out there, but I don't have an analyst on staff to really get the most out of them. Google gives me what I need," relates Davis.

The men's category has increased significantly with this change. People turned from shoppers to buyers as conversion rates have increased by 50 percent—and the value of every page view has increased 65 percent.

Hilfiger is migrating much of its photography to lay-down display as new products come online and low inventory sells out.

Mr. Davis offers this advice to any online marketer: "You need to test to see how your shopper reacts to your product. Tuxedos or swimsuits may be different, but we found out what our customers prefer for men's shirts."

YOUR DOMAIN NAME

How Online Branding Works

THERE ARE FOUR WAYS customers find your company on the web: they search for you specifically; they find you while browsing for related products or services; your website has been referred by a friend via web or email; or they find you "by accident"—when they're on the web looking at, or looking for, something else.

Branding well on the web makes it easier for potential and existing customers to find you and become engaged with you. In this chapter, we'll focus on how to make sure that your customers find *you*—instead of a competitor—when browsing online.

WHAT'S IN A NAME?

Your domain name is more than just your web address—it is your "brand name" in a boundary-free, global nation that has never heard of you. The reason names are used to brand a website is that the name serves as a mnemonic aid for a website's IP (Internet protocol) number. Your actual address is the IP number: for example, 205.134.233.1. But because such strings of numbers aren't easy to remember, the architects of the Internet (which did not include Al Gore) created a Domain Name

System to cross-reference IP numbers with alphanumeric characters. This system is used by Domain Name Servers (DNS) and can serve up your home page's uniform resource locator (URL) at speeds that are a tiny fraction of a second.

It goes without saying that the best domain name is like a good ad slogan: short, snappy, and able to telegraph immediately who you are and what your website offers. It should be easy to type, easy to remember, and—most important these days—visually compact so it can be discernible in a web video or other screen image.

Some of the best-known brands on the web, such as Federal Express and eBay, got their web names by default—they were not a first choice! Shipping industry giant Federal Express was an early mover into the web in the 1980s, a time when the number of letters in a domain name were commonly brief, to help prevent errors in keystroking. It chose to go with the five-letter nickname customers had given its document service: FedEx. An astute choice, and www.fedex.com has become an iconic URL.

Procter & Gamble wasn't so lucky. Special characters like the ampersand are used as coding instructions in html, so are not allowed in domain names, even today. It took years for the detergent and toothpaste manufacturer to even get www.pg.com. It had to be purchased from a company that registered it first. And it took years more for customers to adequately find the brand given its frequent misspellings—one reason why P & G devoted a lot of its early web marketing to expensive banner ads hot-linked to the hard-to-find company website.

As for eBay.com, your authors remember—with some embarrassment—trying to talk founder Pierre Omidyar out of the name—a play on the auction term "abey"—as it was considered too obscure. But, the other domain names we proposed were already taken, so eBay it was.

As the web grew, naming conventions expanded. Federal Express added www.federalexpress.com. And once longer names up to 63 characters long became acceptable, corporations cursed with an ampersand (&) such as Arm & Hammer, Procter & Gamble, Barnes & Noble and others could thus be armandhammer.com, procterandgamble.com, and barnesandnoble.com. By 2000, the Internet was sufficiently mature to allow a wider range of language characters, including Kanji and Arabic scripts, and currently 11 different character sets are being tested for their usefulness.

If you are tasked with choosing a domain name for your company, remember that your obvious first choice may not be the best choice to establish a new brand on the web. Unique words—made-up words—are easier to protect as a trademark and often easier for a customer to recall.

Granted, this has led to some laughable names that have yet to become household words: Squidoo.com (a shopping recommendation site) and jibberjobber.com (career advice for jobseekers). In the business realm, newcomers hope to rise as Xobni.com (an email management company) and Yoomba (an email services provider).

Another trend is longer names that incorporate a slogan or message; this is common to ad-supported blog sites, such as pinkisthenewblog .com (fashion and celebrities).

However—if you've already been successful in obtaining a suitable domain name for your company, don't pat yourself on the back just yet—you aren't done yet, not by a long shot!

FOR SALE: DIRTY DOMAINS DONE DIRT CHEAP

Domains are cheap. That's why they're so expensive.

Anyone with $1.99 can register a domain name on the Internet, through one of several service bureaus established as domain registrars, such as Godaddy.com, Sedo.com, Network Solutions and Yahoo!. You don't have to have a real company, or even put up a website to grab and hold on to a name.

If the rule of commercial real estate is location, location, location, the rule of the Internet is domain, domain, domain. The analogy was completely appropriate to the domain land rush of the late 1990s, which saw the rise of domain brokers, "used domain lots" and "cyber-squatters," who purchased domain names hoping to sell them to businesses that needed them. The practice continues today and many common terms (jewelry.com, gardens.com) were snapped up quickly and have changed hands many times over the years. By the time you've covered all your web assets, registering and purchasing all variations of a name—including misspellings, necessary foreign versions, key product trade names and even your CEO's actual given name—can run into several thousand dollars.

For most organizations, it's well worth it. Thus, Burger King, the hamburger chain, holds the domain names not just for burgerking.com, but for common misspellings like bugerking.com.

It's a mistake to think that as long as you were able to secure .com, you could be reasonably secure in protecting your brand on the web. Today, we see a proliferating use of other top-level domains (TLDs) beyond the original handful such as .org (meant for nonprofits), .edu (for schools), .gov (for government sites) and .net (meant for networks) applied to commercial enterprises. This means that to protect your brand, you'll also have to secure your name in all common TLDs, and in all the newer TLDs that may apply to your industry. If you don't, a competitor or other foe may get hold of it first.

It's also a mistake to think that because you are the owner of a trademarked name in the real world, your claim to the same name online will automatically be given to you in the event of a dispute. Cybersquatters around the world are always looking for opportunities; for example, in early 2007, Google received, and shared, an email it received from an enterprising young man who had secured "Google" in domains the giant search company had actually missed.

While it is true that that Internic (a governing body of the Internet) will generally award a domain that includes a trademark name to the

Figure 3-1 Domain seller

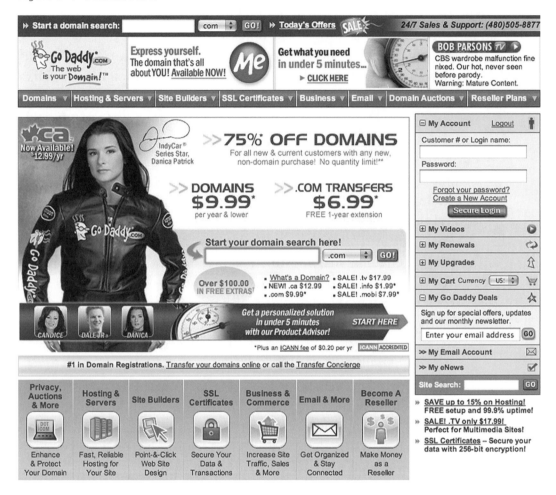

trademark holder, the actual process can take years and can be hotly contested if it's a case of misspelling (the term for this is "typosquatting"). More than an annoyance, typosquatting can steal your customers and hurt your organization's ability to adequately protect a trademarked name.

The U.S. Army and Air Force Exchange Service (AAFES), which

operates a virtual PX merchant site for U.S. armed forces customers and their families (www.aafes.com), actually had to go to WIPO (World Intellectual Property Organization) Arbitration and Mediation to get back www.affes.com from Hong Kong traders Modern Empire Internet Ltd., who had registered this address with registrar eNom in 2001, as a pointer site to a website offering a variety of goods, including military surplus clothing.

While AAFES had trademarked AAFES.com as early as 1998, it didn't catch on to the typosquatter until April 2006, complaining both to Internic and WIPO; it was awarded a legal transfer of the name by June 27, 2006, but as of July 4, 2008, clicking on www.affes.com still took you to the Hong Kong trader site.

Figure 3-2 AAFES.com, the official online service for military families

Figure 3-3 AFFES.com, a typosquatter site

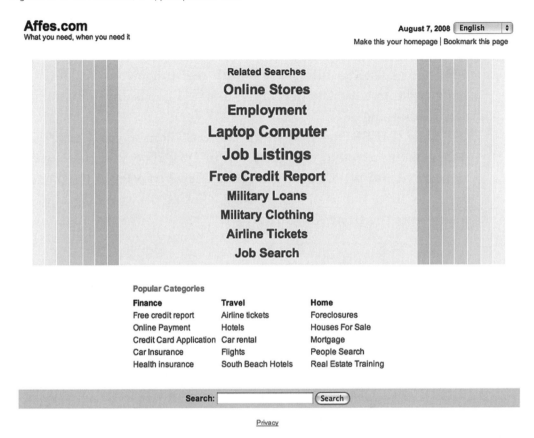

If you enjoy reading legal briefs, this and some important precedent-setting court rulings for international domain name squatting can be found at the following three sites:

www.wipo.int/amc/en/domains/decisions/html/2006/d2006-0510.html

www.wipo.int/amc/en/domains/decisions/html/2000/d2000-0624.html

www.wipo.int/amc/en/domains/decisions/html/2000/d2000-
    0624.html

Everyone else, just be aware that if you challenge a domain squat-
ter in today's world, the response back, if you get one, is "You and what
army?"

COVER YOUR BUTT WITH VARIABLES

Domain names should always be secured in the following top-level
domains:

Mycompany.com

Mycompany.net

Mycompany.org

The TLDs .org and .net have been the most problematic, as they are
often the default of companies who couldn't get the .com designation.
And, these three most common TLDs are often grabbed up by competitors or speculators. The aftermarket in domains continues to attract
prospectors: Pizza.com, registered for $20 in 1994, sold for $2.6 million
at a Zedo auction in April 2008.

In 2000, and again in 2004, an array of new TLDs were introduced
by ICAAN, the international standards organization for Internet names.
Of these, the most useful one is .biz, but others may apply to your business case.

Others and those added since: .aero, .arpa, .cat, .coop, .info, .int, .jobs,
.mobi, .museum, .name, .pro and .travel. One of the more significant new
TLDs is .tel, which may be expected to compete in the wireless mobile
space with .mobi. In June 2008, ICAAN approved a change in rule structure that might add hundreds, or even thousands more TLDs to the mix,

and allow companies to have their own TLDs. For example, Apple or Dell could apply for .mac and .dell.

Even the biggest corporations are still playing catch-up with this. At this writing, Burger King has secured "burgerking" in all known extensions, and "bugerking.net" but still hasn't gotten around to registering "bugerking" in .biz and .edu (still available).

Other variations including adding a hyphen—for example, Bill Gates still hasn't gotten his hands on Micro-soft.com. Securing the name with words transposed (WorldFountain/FountainsWorld) and common Englishisms (colour for color, for example) substituted can offer added protection.

INTERNATIONAL BRANDING—TRY THIS FOR A TWIST

The international community has also broadly embraced two-character "country codes," the TLDs that designate a particular country. If your company has international roots, there is a certain cachet to a European or Asian web address. This is doubly true for a company that merely wishes to borrow such cachet: a business selling Irish wool sweaters, for example, might benefit from a name such as www.irish-sweaters.ie—in addition to www.irishsweaters.com. As the old saying goes, on the Internet no one knows you are a dog—or whether you're fulfilling orders from Killarny or Hackensack.

Here's a page with a handy reference to international country codes: www.webopedia.com/quick_ref/topleveldomains/countrycodeA-E.asp.

Foreign TLDs are also the fallback for companies who came late to the Internet party. Harlequin Enterprises, a global book publishing empire based in Toronto, has yet to gain Harlequin.com as that domain has been in use since 1992 by Global Graphics, a British engineering firm that makes a print server product with Harlequin in its name. Clicking on www.harlequin.com redirects your query to Global Graphic's home page, www.globalgraphics.com. Go there and it's plain to see why Global is holding on to this domain: the website makes it clear that their product lines service the print publishing industry—and it's hoping to grab some "accidental" customers with an interest in book publishing.

A lookup at www.Harlequin.org shows this belongs to a blogger with literary aspirations who registered that domain name in 1998.

In the meantime, Toronto's Harlequin home on the web is www .harlequin.ca, which uses the Canadian country code, registered in 2000, and www.eharlequin.com, a consumer site registered in 1999. Some of the newer TLDs were secured beginning with Harlequin.net in 2000, which is still "under construction"—although we'd recommend it be re-tooled as a pointer page that redirects web traffic to www.eHarlequin.com.

REGISTERING PRODUCT NAMES AND PERSONAL NAMES

Best practice now suggests that establishing a firm brand presence on the web means registering dozens of domain names you will use for nothing else but pointer pages. A pointer page simply redirects web traffic to your main website. Thus, a company may have perhaps only one fully functioning website, but scores of pointer sites that collect browsing web users and direct them successfully to the home site. Compared to the cost of trademarking a product name or business name, the fee is relatively modest if you use discount domain traders.

Another new wrinkle is to register as a domain your own name (if you are a sole proprietor) and/or the names of your company officers or spokespeople. It is standard procedure in the entertainment world— artists, performers, actors, musicians, celebrities and authors—to register personal names in at least the .com. If your marketing plans anticipate that you, or a company principal, will soon be making Page 6 headlines in the *New York Post*, Gawker.com, Smoking Gun or Defamer, or your goal is to get more than 15 minutes of fame, it may be prudent to register a personal name as a .com ahead of time.

Wanna Be on TV?

The suffix ".tv" was originally assigned as the country code for Tuvalu, a small, remote island nation in the Pacific Ocean with a population of about 10,000 people. Shortly after it received the assignment, the government of Tuvalu thought it had a bright idea and started shopping it around, and in 2000 sold the rights to its domain to Idealab, a California venture firm that hoped to develop it as DotTV. The deal called for Idealab to pay Tuvalu up to $50 million over 12 years and a guaranteed $4 million per year for the right to register Internet addresses in the .tv domain.

To recoup the investment, DotTV attempted to auction off names to television industry companies at $1,000 and up. Had the Great Internet Bust of 2001 not intervened, this might have worked. Eventually DotTV was purchased by Verisign, which became its official registrar. In 2006, Verisign and Demand Media (founded by former MySpace chairman Richard Rosenblatt) formed a joint venture to relaunch the .tv TLD to broadcasters on the cusp of new interest in web video and broadband web media. It appears to have been more successful this time around. Last we checked, dottv.com was parked and available on a broker site.

Note: Registrations are an ongoing cost as domain names need to be renewed every two years or so; if not they fall back into the open market for domain names. This can fall under your operating budget or your marketing budgeting, but should be penciled in.

The easy way to discover if a domain name has been taken is to type it into your browser and see what comes up. While this will easily disqualify quite a few names in quite a few TLDs, it is now recommended to take this step on a secure, firewalled computer, and look up a name on a relatively secure registrar, such as Network Solutions or Yahoo! Domains (smallbusiness/yahoo.com/domains), to prevent the preemptive theft of a name through abusive "front-running" (see below).

For generic top-level domains and international codes, you can find appropriate registrars on the site of the Internet Corporation for Assigned Names and Numbers (ICANN), the nonprofit organization that keeps track of all the names.

If some names appropriate to you are already taken, the next step is to look up a domain name in WHOIS, on a secure registrar's site. Whois information includes the contact information for the owner of the name, including address and phone number, plus the IP address and location of the host name server. It also shows when the name was assigned, when it was last transferred (if applicable) and when it may expire. Law enforcement organizations use the Whois database, and it is useful for trademark housekeeping—searching Whois to find out if someone is using a variant of your trademarked name, and keeping up to date on expirations and renewals.

STAY AHEAD OF FRONT RUNNERS, CYBERSQUATTERS AND TYPOSQUATTERS

Researching on a secure, firewalled computer may help you avoid the problem of "front running." Front running is when a cybersquatter registers a name just after—sometimes just minutes after—someone else has conducted a domain name search on a registrar's site, performed a WHOIS query on Network Solutions or typed a domain in his or her browser to see if there is an active website. How do front runners know what you're doing? Front runners get their tips sent automatically by their Internet service providers, by spyware stuck on your computer or by the very domain registry you may be using to register other domains. Front runners may then set up a single-page site to try to attract pay-per-click ads in your business category, or will resell the domain—to you or one of your direct competitors—at a substantially higher price than $1.99.

Domain snoopers—and even some domain registrars themselves—

preemptively registering a domain just after you have conducted a domain name search is a contentious issue. Network Solutions has come under the gun since its January 2008 announcement that it would "reserve" a name that was searched in its website for four days, as a "customer protection" to prevent front running. During the four-day period, the name is not considered active; the customer who has inquired thus has four days to search again on Network Solutions only, in order to obtain the name. If not purchased by the inquiring customer within four days, the name is made available again and essentially up for grabs.

According to Network Solutions, "this protection measure provides our customers with the opportunity to register domains they have previously searched for without fear that the name will be already taken through Front Running." While this does not sit well with many who believe in free trade and open markets on the web, most registrars are adopting similar forms of "protection" to make the process of domain name exploration more comfortable for users and more lucrative for their respective registries.

WHICH REGISTRAR IS BEST?

Registration of domain names was deregulated and decentralized in 2000 with the following organizations supervising the most common TLDs. Verisign, which has managed over the years to become more or less the "Good Housekeeping Seal"™ of Internet commerce (much to the dismay of Good Housekeeping, we are sure) is "accredited" by ICANN to register names in .com, for example, although many other commercial firms have the right to register most of the original TLDs. According to Verisign, more than 60 million names are registered in the .com domain.

Here is the full list of ICANN's accredited "specialty" domain registrars:

- *.aero* (reserved for the global aviation community), sponsored by Societé Internationale de Telecommunications Aeronautiques SC (SITA)

- *.asia* (reserved for the Pan-Asia and Asia Pacific region), sponsored by DotAsia Organisation

- *.biz* (restricted to businesses), operated by NeuLevel

  .cat (reserved for the Catalan linguistic and cultural community), sponsored by Fundació puntCat

- *.com*, operated by Verisign Global Registry Services

- *.coop* (reserved for cooperatives), sponsored by Dot Cooperation LLC

- *.info*, operated by Afilias Limited

- *.jobs* (reserved for the human resource management community), sponsored by EmployMedia LLC, operated by Afilias Limited

- *.mobi* (reserved for consumers and providers of mobile products and services), sponsored by mTLD Top Level Domain, Ltd.

- *.museum* (restricted to museums and related persons), sponsored by the Museum Domain Management Association (MuseDoma)

- *.name* (restricted to individuals), operated by Global Name Registry

- *.net*, operated by Verisign Global Registry Services

- *.org*, operated by Public Interest Registry

- *.pro* (restricted to licensed professionals), operated by RegistryPro

- .travel (reserved for entities whose primary area of activity is in the travel industry), sponsored by Tralliance Corporation.

Several hundred more domain registrars, most of them basically "domain name brokers" and proprietors of "used domain lots," are also accredited, and their contact information may be found online by searching ICANN's link: www.icann.org/registrars/accreditation-qualified-list.html.

PURCHASING THROUGH DOMAIN BROKERS

For many years, Network Solutions (www.netsol.org) was considered the only legitimate registrar, as it was itself a commercial spinoff of ICANN. Today it is a full-service web hosting company, highly competitive in price, and trying its best to stay one step ahead of both legitimate and unsavory registration firms.

We do not make any recommendation for any firm; in general your organization should look at value and reputation. If you have a lot of variables to register, competitive pricing will also figure largely.

Recapturing an existing domain can be accomplished by making a bid (usually anonymous) through that domain's registrar. In some cases it may seem wise to simply contact the domain owner directly. Naturally it would make sense to establish ahead of time the amount of money you're willing to part with to gain the domain, and at which point you are ready to walk away.

To make an opening bid for a used domain, check the Whois information for how long the domain has been held. Since many cybersquatters work on volume, start with a low price that will cover the costs of registration (and renewals) plus a little more.

Domain speculators are certainly a peculiar bunch, and they are global. Among them is Rob Monster, chairman of GoLife Mobile Corporation and managing director of Monster Venture Partners (www.monsterventure.com), an early-stage venture capital firm based in Seattle. While we disagree with his claim that domain speculators can reap "substantial wealth" by hogging and selling, here is his take on the current ebb and flow of domain name transactions:

So who owns all these domains? Well, to a very large extent, the domains are held by Domainers. The first generation of domainers was comprised largely of speculators who pursued domain acquisition with little interest in developing the domains. A number of these domainers amassed substantial wealth through a combination of recurring income from a practice called "domain parking" as well as periodic windfalls from domain resale, often to other domain speculators but also to developers, private equity and even public equity markets. To date, very few of the domainers have been focused on domain development. Most of the domainers who tried their hand at development turned out to be not very good at it and so they went back to the easy money of domain parking until the lucky (and rare) day when a buyer emerges with a viable bid.

My personal view is that the market for domain names is on the cusp of becoming far more sophisticated. Parked domains that offer limited utility will become progressively less likely to be indexed by search engines, making it more difficult to arbitrage the cost—acquisition price plus cumulative maintenance costs—relative to the advertising revenue from parking the domain.

Used domains can also be found on "drop lists"—the names of domains whose registration has expired because the owner failed to renew properly. Here is Rob Monster on drop lists:

> One of my favorite places to look for domains is TDNAM.com, an affiliate of GoDaddy . . . Click on the expired tab and just troll the list for a few hours. Most of the domains are not development worthy, but if you are methodical, you can uncover a few good ones every day for an acquisition price of $10–15.

If you have inherited or are trying to fix a web property, registrar drop lists are also a good place to check to make sure your organization's domains have not expired for lack of care.

BRANDING IN CHINA

No matter what you may be selling, your business in China should be enormous,
if the Chinese who should buy your goods would only do so.

CARL CROW, IN *400 MILLION CUSTOMERS* (1937)

The now 1.3 billion (population) question today remains as it did in Crow's time: whether the country is a potential mass market for western brands (and seasoned online marketers), or a golden illusion?

Global Internet giants (eBay, Yahoo!, Google, etc.) have yet to dominate the Chinese online market. Once known for the C2C model (aka "Copy to China"), speed and innovation of China's local players have reshaped the market. Market shares for search, instant messenger and online auctions experienced high volatility in recent years with local players Baidu, TenCent and Alibaba rising to the top. Branding your product in this fast-moving marketplace starts with knowing who the key players are.

On China's Baidu the top search result is usually an ad, as Baidu displays paid search ads prior to natural results while maintaining positive user, advertiser and analyst feedback. While Google remains a formidable, experienced challenger, Baidu is China's search giant (65 percent market share) and continues to expand from its core strength in search engine results publishing into user-generated Q&A communities, online auctions and display.

Together with paid search, display is expected to account for 97 percent of China's $2.7 billion online advertising market in 2010. Leveraging thousands of sales distributors (known as "resellers"), Search is reaching local advertisers with a relatively new and inexpensive entry point to online marketing that is expected to grow by more than 50 percent annually through 2010.

Display dollars are dominated by China's three major portals Sina, Sohu and NetEase and surprise newcomer, TenCent. No need to pull out your calculator or global CPM (clicks per thousand) rates as these highly visited web destinations continue to price ads on a fixed cost per day basis to reach China's large brand advertisers, who are more schooled in traditional media (TV, print, etc.) pricing models.

Built on the strength of its dominant QQ instant messaging community, TenCent has quietly become one of China's leading Internet success stories. China's IM user penetration is roughly 86 percent (vs. 39 percent in the United States), which translates into more engagement opportunities for marketers, and as such, 2007 witnessed TenCent become a leading player in brand advertising, online entertainment and e-commerce.

While demand for informational and transactional related content is growing, entertainment remains the leader. Unlike downloading MP3s or movies, casual and multi-player online games (MMORPG) can attract up to one million concurrent customers. Think online applications, in this case games, renting for $0.25/hour and you can see why China's Internet cafés have become the arcades of a new generation.

Some, like Shanda, leveraged their strength in online gaming to make inroads into online advertising, home entertainment and even redefining the online gaming business model from paying to play to a highly profitable free to play model—instead making money off virtual items and community tools.

Trying to describe China's online market in 500 words or less one cannot hope to capture the story whole; instead the above shares but a few examples and observations of what should be a dynamic, high growth market for years to come.

—T. R. Harrington, Cofounder and CEO, DarwinMarketing.com

PART II
ATTRACTING
CUSTOMERS

SEARCH ENGINE MARKETING

Optimize and Win

SEARCH ENGINES JUMP-START the process of engagement for new customers who have never heard of you, and also for existing customers who may be researching several options online for a specific business need.

The active web seeker is halfway to a qualified prospect. So, how do customers find *your* business? Shockingly, it's still a hit-or-miss approach. A 2008 global study of 2007 fourth-quarter online shopping by Nielsen Online found that among consumers, two-thirds will go to a site they already know. But, a full one-third will use a search engine or "randomly surf" before selecting an online store. This is important because even B-to-B customers typically use the same online behaviors in the office as they do at home.

While the study also showed the importance of special offers (banners or email advertising) and peer-to-peer marketing (review sites and word of web applications) the tendency to random surfing behaviors keeps the spotlight on search strategies as the best method to reach the larger web audience that has no idea you even exist.

According to eMarketer, over the next four years a solid 40 percent

67

Figure 4-1 How users find web merchant sites

Shopping Site Selection Method (Global Average, Percent of Online Purchasers in Past Three Months)	
Selection Method	% of Online Purchasers
Regular purchase site	60%
Surfing	33
Search engine	31
Special offer	30
Recommendation	23
Shopping comparison	23
Regular offline store	20
Online review	18
Online advertising	14
TV, print or other advertising	11
Other	6

Source: The Nielsen Company

of all online ad spending will be spent on paid search. Sadly, only a small fraction of promotional spending dollars will be spent tuning up a website, an organizational news release, or a streaming video ad with search engine optimization (SEO) techniques. Why is this sad? *Because SEO is the only way to get the maximum impact from all the other dollars you spend online.*

Search is probably the most misunderstood tool for online marketing, and yet it remains popular with online marketers in much the same way email is popular. It's quantifiable, fits into any budget, and appears to give good results. A survey of 2,000 email clients by the email services company Datatran found that, while 80 percent of them perceived that email was their strongest performing tool, slightly over 70 percent had equally high confidence in search engine marketing over display ads (37 percent)

Figure 4-2 Datatron survey of marketer confidence

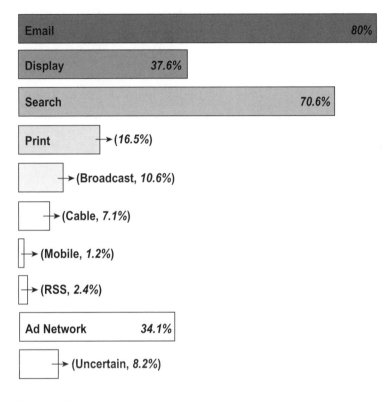

Email	80%
Display	37.6%
Search	70.6%
Print	→(16.5%)
	→(Broadcast, 10.6%)
	→(Cable, 7.1%)
	→(Mobile, 1.2%)
	→(RSS, 2.4%)
Ad Network	34.1%
	→(Uncertain, 8.2%)

Source: Datatron.com

when answering the question, "Which advertising media buys perform strongly for your company?" (Note: Multiple answers were allowed).

Yes, search is a star performer. But, perhaps, not in the way you think.

HOW SEARCH IS LIKE A STAR BASKETBALL PLAYER

To tell you why search is the Antawn Jamison of Marketing, first we have to tell you who Antawn Jamison is. Antawn Jamison is an all-star

NBA player for the Washington Wizards. In 2007 he led his team into the playoffs, an unheard-of occurrence for the lowly Wizards, and helped them into the first round again in 2008. What is relatively unique about Jamison is the nature of his game. He's not a dominant center, like Shaquille O'Neil, or a flashy shooting guard like Michael Jordan. Instead he's a team player who does the dirty work close to the basket, tipping in a teammate's errant shot, gobbling up rebounds and converting them to baskets. Do you get the concept?

Search is just like that. Where most media is aimed at creating demand, search media does the dirty work of converting that demand to sales, leads or any other metric you want to track. If a search campaign is properly planned, it is able to "tip in" the inquiry that came to the misremembered tag line or the misspelled brand name. It can be the Antawn Jamison of the marketing team, turning the good work of others on the team into sales. Converting the close miss into a basket.

But organizations driven by sales, like the NBA teams, hunger for flashier players. Stars like Michael Jordan. Jordan is the equivalent of the 30-second TV spot, still the glamour boy of the marketing mix, pulling down the big bucks. But, increasingly, both basketball and marketing are becoming true "team" games. Every campaign should utilize search as its secret weapon, its Antawn Jamison, and show respect for the ability to do the dirty work of converting shots to scores (or searches to sales).

SEARCH AND DISPLAY: A WINNING COMBINATION

An interesting survey done by Yahoo! in 2006 sought to measure the individual and collective impact of paid search and banner advertising. It uncovered some interesting data in three sectors: travel sites, retail sites, and telecom service sites.

In all cases, the test was Internet-wide and matched a control group to select groups that were exposed to either "just search" advertising, display advertising, and both types of advertising on the same screen environment.

Yahoo!'s conclusion was that, while display ads were helpful in getting more visitors to a website (about 4 percent increase from the control group), a search ad could get more visitors (over 50 percent increase). The visitation level boosted to 68 percent when Web surfers saw both a display ad and a search ad they could click through.

Search also beat display only in terms of a lift in online purchasing—an amazing 210 percent increase versus 50 percent increase from the display ads. While both methods showed that any form of web ad exposure boosts your website's sales (no surprise there), online purchasing increased 244 percent when audiences were exposed to both search and display.

And, those of you responsible for brick-and-mortar sales channels, please note: the study also tracked offline (i.e., store, catalog and telephone) sales. Display web ads were credited with a minor 9 percent lift in offline sales, while search-only was credited with a robust 42 percent increase in offline sales. The combination of search and display advertising on the web was found to boost offline sales by 89 percent compared to the control group.

This is only some of the research reinforcing the resurgence of banner advertising on the web. While click-through rates on banner ads have improved, they still remain low (averaging 0.25 percent). Despite this, it's pretty much a given that web exposure increases brand awareness and brand recall when a customer is ready to buy. Search ads arguably pull more qualified website visitors since that customer is actively searching, not passively browsing. But the combination can be powerful, especially if you have a new product or relatively unknown brand in need of exposure.

Search marketing provides the most level playing field for messaging across the globe. Any organization, nonprofit or individual can participate in search and SEO.

BEST PRACTICES FOR SEO AND SEM

Search engine lookup dates to the dawn of Internet time. Even today, an estimated 50 percent of all Internet activity involves looking something up—"searching." Search engine manipulation—all right, let's call it "search engine optimization"—became a priority for us at Cybernautics in 1995, and later a specialty.

In hard terms, search engine optimization (SEO) became a priority for every web marketer as soon as it was realized that Internet users, like most of humanity, are inherently lazy. When someone types a search phrase into a search engine—"how to buy a ski boot" into the lozenge-shaped search box on Yahoo! or MSN.com, even in the early years dozens of screen pages would appear, revealing tens of thousands of answers to the query. But the user would eventually tire of scrolling through the many pages of relevant and irrelevant results. And, it was discovered, some 85 percent of users would never make it past the first search page, and its ten or so listings or URLs. An iProspect white paper study in 2006 upped that figure to 90 percent, so clicking beyond the first page is still a rare occurrence. Getting on the first search page first became an art, then a science, and today, it's an industry. At the height of the Internet's first boom, Steve Diorio, marketing guru whose clients have included IBM, Hewlett-Packard and Eastman Chemical, made this observation:

> The disciplines required can be described as "white magic," "black magic" and "green magic."
>
> White magic is the accepted practice of building a web page's hidden source code with certain keywords and phrases, for the benefit of search engine spiders, automated search programs that file and rank web sites by the relevant content. This is basic procedure for any web site. Tactics include analyzing the source code of a successful competitor's web pages to help identify the most effective keywords . . .

Black magic is a borderline discipline. The proprietary algorithms used by search engines to automate ranking can be rigged, or at least reverse-engineered to artificially raise position . . . This discipline is likely to have a limited life as search engines continue to adopt pay-for-placement ranking models.

That's what green magic is all about: businesses that pay the largest fee to certain search engines will be given the number-one positions. Green magic is good news for marketers; there are always going to be opportunities to buy your way to the top of a listing page. (*Source*: *Beyond E*, by Steven Diorio, McGraw-Hill, New York, 2002.)

THE BASICS OF SEO: ON-PAGE AND OFF-PAGE OPTIMIZATION

Search has grown up from the early years from the first search engines—Yahoo!, Lycos and AOL—to the point where every commercial shopping website, every publishing website, and in fact nearly every website employs a "search box" to help the visitor quickly locate a topic, posting or product. Searches within an organization's website are based usually only on key words that can be typed in. That's fine once your customer has arrived at your website; it's getting them there from the search aggregators—Yahoo!, Google, MSN and AOL—that's gotten harder and harder, given the billions of pages that can be searched.

Prior to the emergence of Google in 1998, searches on the aggregate engines were typically "organic"—type in a phrase or group of words, and the results were solely based on "on-page" factors like keyword density—the number of times a searchable phrase appears within the source code of a web page—and metadata or metatags. These are the HTML coding that describes the content of a web page; it's inserted into the source code but usually not visible to anyone viewing the page. Theoretically this classic best practice helps the search engine discover the most relevant result to a search query, with the more specific phrase ("Where to buy Solomon size 8 men's X Wave red ski boots in Idaho?")

Figure 4-3 *The beauty of search*

> ## Salomon Xwave 8 (2004)
>
> Ridden 1 1/2 seasons, in good condition size 28.0. Would like to get about \$100-\$150, but am flexible.
>
> Contact Chester at (555) 555-5555 or email cheter04@ooo.com

returning a highly specific answer (an actual January 2008 classified ad in an Idaho newspaper selling the exact boot, used).

Elegant, and effective. So what's wrong with this picture? First, as we've said, people are lazy. Of the approximately 10 billion searches performed by American Internet users each month, very few are likely to be so specific.

Second, what is beneficial to the customer may be anathema to a marketer—there must be at least a dozen ski shops in Idaho—and many more websites—panting to sell, if not this exact ski boot, a newer model ski boot, or some kind of ski boot or accessory ski stuff to Mr. Size 8.

In the middle lies opportunity—and exploiting that opportunity is the soul of search. Getting *your* company to that first results page is *still* a priority for every web marketer.

KEY FACTORS OF SEARCH

A major Google innovation, now followed by the industry, was to also utilize "off-page" factors, preeminently the number and importance of inbound links. The more links from other websites you have, the better your ranking on most search engines.

SEO practitioners therefore not only optimize metadata and workarounds for Flash and Javascript coding (which are difficult for spiders to recognize), but also must support other online marketing efforts, such as a drive to recruit inbound links through affiliate networks (see Chapter 7). Having a strong affiliate network, and reaching out with publicity and promotion to blogs and news sites (see Chapter 8) are two proven methods to increase the number of inbound links, and hence to improve rankings.

It was interesting to note that an April 2007 survey of common factors affecting rankings showed that, ten years later, keywords, metatags and popularity as measured by inbound links are still the most important factors to address in order to improve rank and page position.

Top 10 Positive Factors

1. Keyword use in title tag
2. Anchor text of inbound link
3. Global link popularity of site
4. Age of site
5. Link popularity within the site's internal link structure
6. Topical relevance of inbound links to site
7. Link popularity of site in topical community
8. Keyword use in body text
9. Global link popularity of linking site
10. Topical relationship of linking page

Currently, Google weights or ranks results based on more than 200 "signals" or classifications. Google and the other two major search engines, Yahoo! and MSN Live Search, constantly revamp the algorithms they use to assign ranking, keeping one step ahead of the "black magic" or "black hat" methods to jigger rankings to unfair advantage, such as "keyword stuffing" and "linkspamming"—practices that today can get your URL banned from many search engines' databases.

The latest wrinkle in search is visual search—not just words, but images, and this has proven to be the frontier for cutting-edge advantages in marketing. There is room for creativity in visual search, but for the majority of marketers, dishing out dollars is the only guaranteed method to hit the top of a search page.

SEM—THE EMPIRES OF PAID SEARCH

While SEO is about what you can do to improve your search results, SEM (search engine marketing) is about what search engines can do for you—for a price, of course. AOL may have pioneered the idea of paid search, back when it introduced the concept of buying "keywords" such as "car" or "book" to advertisers such as Ford and Barnes & Noble, but Google popularized "paid search" with its Adwords program, allowing advertisers to pay for ranking under specific keywords.

We like Steve Diorio's definition of paid search as "green magic." As opposed to the "white magic" of creative search terms, and the "black magic" of deliberate rank gaming, the "green magic" of paid search requires no teams of highly creative html programmers. All you need to do is come up with the "green"—and pay a search engine to drift your website URL up into the first page of a search.

You still need to come up with some search terms, though. And that's getting tougher, as the inventory of high-performance terms has shrunk with high demand. This has allowed search engines such as Google and Yahoo! to make millions if not billions of dollars as they charge, typically by the penny, for paid search.

Major advertisers once bit the bullet and paid as much as $500,000 to buy a keyword on AOL. Today, that same advertiser may spend $50,000 for paid search on Google and gain similar results. The good news for the smaller enterprise is that you can compete for the same customers with as little as $1,000, and hijack enough of them to make the exercise worthwhile.

BIDDING TECHNOLOGIES AVAILABLE FOR MAXIMIZING PAID SEARCH

Google and Yahoo! may be the most popular paid search engines but there are more to explore, including highly effective, targeted engines for Local Search, Mobile Search and Vertical Search, included in a list at the end of this chapter.

The Google formula, now adopted by other engines including Yahoo!, bases ranking not just on the auction price one is willing to pay but also on the CTR (click-through rate), which is said to make results more relevant.

There are several technologies that automate the laborious task of bidding on paid search keywords.

These can be divided into rules-based systems such as that offered by Atlas and DoubleClick and portfolio-based systems such as that offered by Efficient Frontier and others. The rules-based systems utilize specific instructions at the keyword level. The portfolio approach actually incorporates stock market theory to manage large numbers of keywords on a macro level.

Today it is nothing for a company to purchase and manage as many as 3 million keywords, as we discuss in our case study below.

Tools and Key Suppliers for SEO and SEM Automation

- *Google Analytics:* Free analysis software available to participants in the Google Adwords program. The "Starter Edition" is an obvious choice for bootstrappers and is also a useful training tool for executives interested in learning about campaign automation.

- *Semphonic:* CampaignTracker from Semphonic (www.semphonic
  .com) provides pay-per-click (PPC) and competitive reporting
  about SEM campaigns. The PPC reports are built using campaign
  data extracted from the search engines. Report data is then
  consolidated into a single Excel report. Competitive reports are
  built by scanning Google and Yahoo! for all the sites that are
  shown organically or in the paid listing for a given list of search
  terms and include who is buying what. Competitive reports help
  reveal the activities of individual competitors, and reports on
  competitor ad copy that may be working better than yours.

- *Enquisite:* Enquisite (www.enquisite.com) of Vancouver, BC,
  Canada, made a major update to their Search Metrics Reporting
  Tool, an analytics system that uses passive objective data culling.
  According to CEO Richard Zwicky, this has a twofold advantage:
  first, because it gathers data passively, users are not penalized for
  using it as it does not spam search engines, and second, it allows
  users to drill down through organic and PPC data ranked under
  phrase, search engine, country, region, city and even zip code.

- *Inceptor:* Inceptor (www.inceptor.com) has a range of tools tailored
  to small businesses, larger companies and interactive agencies. All
  of these allow bidding to be managed in a rules-based environment.
  They also offer Inceptor Word of Net, a visibility and ranking report
  generator.

- *Omniture:* Omniture (www.omniture.com) is one of several companies moving laterally into the search space with a suite of tools
  for business-to-business use. Their product, Search Center, offers
  a standard range of bid management options as well as competitor analysis reporting. Among other features are click-fraud
  analysis and tight integration with Omniture's web-analytics
  package.

- *WebSideStory:* WebSideStory rounded out its ActiveMarketingSuite
  with WebSideStory Bid, a new keyword management solution, and

continued to improve its popular web analytics product, HBX Analytics 3.0. The 2008 purchase of this company by Omniture, indicates a trend for analytics providers to deliver a comprehensive package for their online customers.

- *Eyeblaster:* Eyeblaster (www.eyeblaster.com) has a suite of tools for search called eb.search. To power eb.search, Eyeblaster formed an alliance with The Technology Works, whose suite of tools had only been available in Europe and Asia. In the North American market and in Australia, eb.search can be used either by integrating Eyeblaster's digital ad server or by using eb.search as a stand-alone system. In other markets, eb.search is only available as an integrated offering.

SOME NEW IDEAS FOR SEARCH "CREATIVE" IN SEM

Search marketing is a limited creative discipline charged with a very big job—helping customers find your site when they don't know you, but are specifically looking for the product or service you provide. The title in a Google ad can only be 25 characters long, and the lines in the body of that ad can only have 35 characters. This means you can't say very much; it reduces the "creative" (the ad copy) to a modern equivalent of the Burma Shave ads found along highways long ago.

And the traditional ad elements such as a value proposition and a call to action still have to be there. It's still advertising, even if with a limited palette. For companies used to the information-packed modules of radio minutes, TV spots and magazine ad space, Google advertising can mean a deliberate and drastic step back to simpler and urgently telegraphic communications. Think bumper sticker and billboard. But unlike those, you don't have the leisure of miles going by while the prospective customer views, and absorbs, your ad message. In the web environment of a Google ad, or in fact any search ad, you've only got a fraction of a second to capture the attention of your customer while they are in searching mode.

Success means being slightly more devious and counterintuitive. One recent search campaign stands out for its creativity.

RPA Has Fun—and Sells Cars Too

RPA's strategic 2005–2008 campaign for the Honda Element—a chunky sports utility vehicle—generated a lot of buzz. Search was used, along with actual billboards and a website (automobiles.honda.com/element-and friends), to encourage viewers to interact with a group of adorable critters that included a possum, a platypus, a talking crab and a lizard. While this sounds pretty stupid, the cartoonlike "island" setting was a good call for a young, male audience familiar with gaming sites and Second Life—and bear in mind the vehicle had first been introduced in 2003 and needed a fresh look. The billboards directed drivers to tune into local radio frequencies that played a continuous loop of advertisements that were themselves loopy—the car chatting with the platypus, for example—and also directed to the website.

What got everyone really exited, though, was how this campaign employed search advertising. From a search perspective, the agency focused on buying inexpensive keywords like "possum" and "lizard." These words were far cheaper than terms related to automobiles or Hondas. Of course, the more traditional words were bought as well. But with "Honda element" at $1.15 on Google and "possum" at 10 cents, it is easy to see the benefit of expanding keywords beyond the likeliest suspects.

So did the search part of the campaign deliver?

According to RPA, the search portion of the budget accounted for nearly 40 percent of responses, despite having a budget share that barely made it into double digits. RPA's Mike Margolin ran the search effort and credits Google optimizers and the Yahoo! "buzz" tool with helping make the campaign a success. Overall, search drove traffic that was comparable to what would have been expected from home page takeovers. Margolin noted that the animal-related keywords did not bring in the lion's share of traffic, but, at an average of 10 to 15 cents per click, were much less expensive than car-related words.

Of course, the entire campaign had a high fun quotient. The microsite incorporates an online game in which visitors drive a Honda around an island and can have conversations with the critters. But it is not often that search gets to join in the fun. By buying words outside the car sector (they also bought words like "funny," "freaky" and "hairy"), RPA and Honda extended the spirit of the campaign to search, and those search ads (according to their research) helped lift awareness, brand favorability and purchase intent. And think about it: the only competition they had for "possum" keywords were pest exterminators and T-shirt merchants.

LEGAL ISSUES OF PAID SEARCH

There are unexpected legal issues that have affected search: *GEICO* v. *Google* exemplifies one of them.

The insurance company that has both Warren Buffet and a dancing gecko shilling for it sued Google for having allowed competing insurers to buy the GEICO mark as a keyword. The claim was based on the Lanham Act, a part of the Trademark Code. GEICO asserted that its trademark rights were being violated both by the sale of the marks but also by the use of those marks in the competitor's ads.

In December 2004 the U. S. Federal Court for the Eastern District of Virginia held that Google was within its rights to sell trademarked names as keywords, but allowed that the issue of liability for damages from the use of the GEICO mark in the competitor's ads could go to jury trial. In a written opinion released in August 2005, the Court reiterated and expanded on its December decision that GEICO failed to produce sufficient evidence to establish that the competing advertisements violated the Lanham Act, even though Google's advertising program enables those ads to appear when a user searches on GEICO's trademarks. But the Court also held that the use of GEICO's trademarks in the heading or text of advertisements that appear when a user searches on "GEICO" *does* violate the Lanham Act. The judge gave the parties 30 days to settle and GEICO and Google came to an undisclosed settlement on the 30th day—leaving Google free to continue to sell competitive brand keywords.

Sellers of keywords no doubt breathed a sigh of relief when this case came to conclusion. For sellers of online advertising, the GEICO case had removed concern that existed about the sudden shrinkage of effective inventory that would result from ending competitor bidding on trademarked keywords. Search engines are making a mint on this, although Google and the other search engine organizations will not disclose what percentage this type of keyword bidding represents of inventory and sales. It is clear that it is substantial. The practice has been analogized by proponents as equivalent to erecting a billboard across the street from your competitor's store— nasty but legal—and as out and out trademark infringement by detractors. In a search world already short of inventory, the last thing the web market needs is a sudden shrinkage of high-performance words.

The last thing you need, however, is another headache caused by a competitor poaching your trademark or trade names with impunity. Stealing a march on your competitor's likely keywords remains a gray area. The GEICO case is important because it took place within a Federal Court District (Eastern Virginia) that was known informally as the "rocket docket" for the speed with which cases were resolved there. Because of this, the GEICO case was simply the first suit against Google on this issue to get to Court. But there are other cases that will soon get to Court and raise again the issue of Google's advertising policies regarding trademarks.

In the meantime, best practice suggests that companies be alert to establish and protect their trade names and trademarks. As we discussed in Chapter 3, registering a domain name for all likely variations of your trademarked company name would be a good start. Registering domain names for a specific product or mascot might also be considered.

In the *GEICO* v. *Google* case, the federal judge dismissed a key charge against Google—that consumers were confused by competitors' ads that appear under the GEICO keyword. GEICO's lead lawyer, Charles Ossola, has pointed out that the judge did not expressly condone Google's practice of selling trademarked words to competitors but more narrowly ruled that GEICO had not adequately proved that confusion existed. The judge also ruled that ads that themselves mentioned the GEICO name did violate trademark.

INTERNATIONAL SEM

Increasingly, companies are finding a need to do search advertising on an international basis. This presents special problems in working with the engines and in crafting effective copy.

Google campaigns can be managed globally from a single interface while Yahoo! generally requires contact with local Yahoo! offices. Google has even larger market share outside the United States than within, controlling nearly 70 percent of all search activity outside of North America.

An issue that seems minor but problematic is that in some languages it takes longer words to express the same thought that is shorter in English. This is a large issue with German and Dutch language campaigns. Even though the words are longer, the character number allowed is the same around the world, making normal translation issues even more challenging.

In some countries there are dominant local search engines giving Google a run for its money. This is especially true in China where www.baidu.com is kicking Google's butt.

LOCAL SEARCH

This is a segment of search enjoying strong growth, and there is lots going on. "Local search" is often described as geographically targeted advertising. Enabled by overriding technologies such as global positioning and global mapping, local search allows an advertiser to concentrate on only those searching from a market area, such as a particular town or city, or a particular country or continent. These can be customers who live in the area, or travelers visiting from elsewhere.

Research firm Borrell Associates estimates that local paid search will total $1.8 billion this year, and that, by 2010, geo-targeted email and paid local search will together represent 50 percent of online local advertising. They predict the overall local online market will be nearly $10 billion by then. They also expect a 32 percent increase in geo-targeted advertising online, growing to $7.7 billion by next year. The firm identifies real estate and cars as the local ad category leaders, making up a third of all locally targeted online advertising dollars.

These projections make sense, as rising gas prices in the United States suggest that both businesses and consumers will be purchasing closer to home. That a major dictionary declared "locavore" to be its word of the year—denoting someone who is motivated to shop (especially for food) locally—is an indication of cultural trends also building the audience for local search. Web entrepreneurs are already in this game: National 1-A, which purchased www.pizza.com for $2.6 million, has since built a site that locates the nearest pie joint—make that the nearest *advertiser's* pie joint—when you type in your zip code.

Microsoft, as part of its launch of Windows Live Search, recently unveiled a local search function that lets users see cities from a 45-degree "bird's-eye view" of a particular map location. The mapping feature currently covers 30 percent of the United States and 100 cities worldwide. Derrick Connell, MSN's search business general manager, says that local searches account for 15 to 20 percent of online queries.

DexOnline, owned by RH Donnelly, claims to have generated the most local online searches, at least in its 14-state region. The company says that it generated almost twice as many searches as the next closest competitors—in order, Yahoo!, SuperPages, Google Local and Yellow-Pages.com. Newer features include draggable maps and map-based search, comparison-shopping pages, user-generated itineraries for multistop shopping and personal contact lists to help consumers build personalized online yellow pages.

LocalLaunch, an SEO/SEM firm focused on local search, has also been acquired by RH Donnelly, which is the third largest U.S. publisher of yellow pages on the print side. This follows the purchase of Inceptor by SuperPages and ClickForward by Yellow Book, leaving Yellow-Pages.com (parent company ATT) as the only major U.S. yellow pages publisher who has not bought an SEM company.

Yelp.com, which started out in the San Francisco Bay Area, is now rolling out nationally. It has more than 100,000 user-generated reviews and more than a million unique visitors per month. In the last few months Yelp has established a presence in New York, Boston, Chicago, Los Angeles and Seattle. The site combines MySpace-like profiles and community with local business and entertainment content.

Angie's List, which has launched a national PR and advertising campaign, has a format similar to *Consumer Reports* and a "consumer pays" business model. It began in the Southeast about 10 years ago and competes with Kudzu, Citysearch, Yelp, Judy's Book, InsiderPages, Yahoo! Local and Zipingo.

Yokel competes with NearbyNow, ShopLocal, Become, CNET and Froogle in the local shopping sector. The site has recently expanded to the San Francisco Bay Area, offering an expanded number of retailers and "Best of the Bay" winners. In the local shopping category, sites are offering various combinations of local info and shopping and inventory data to make it easy for users to find products at nearby stores.

Backfence differs from other local sites in that it offers not just community, but also local news. It has formally launched initial service for cities in Maryland and Virginia as well as for Silicon Valley.

VERTICAL SEARCH

Vertical search is an area in considerable ferment. Much venture capital funding has flowed to the area, under the assumption that the big search players are so broad that there is opportunity for sites devoted to specific niches. There is plenty of evidence to suggest that web users may well flock to niche search engines—Amazon.com, after all, is at heart a powerful search engine for looking up books in print that serves results from keywords and then directs consumers to online retailers selling new books, as well as individuals selling used editions.

A JupiterResearch study identifies four primary vertical categories that would be likely to account for the majority of spending: retail, financial services, travel and media and entertainment. But many other niches are getting funding.

Here are some examples of vertical search:

Travel

Besides Expedia, Orbitz and Priceline, there are already many competitors in this vertical, including SideStep, Mobissimo and FareChase.

Kayak (www.kayak.com), which has been around for a while, launched a $10 million TV ad campaign with user-generated videos from its core audience of young male travelers. Newcomer Farecast has sophisticated technology that looks at pricing, scheduling and availability (among 115 indicators) to predict prices on specific flights and thereby give travelers an idea of when to book in order to get the best price. Farecast predicts whether fares will rise or fall over the next seven days. It also provides a fare history chart so users can see fluctuations and the average lowest price over the last 45 to 90 days. The company claims to have made over 90 billion airfare observations to build the predictions. Like other vertical travel search sites, Farecast displays links to book directly at airline websites. Farecast launched with flights departing only from Boston and Seattle, but will roll out other departure cities over the course of the year.

Another new player in the travel vertical is FareCompare, which aims to empower consumers with flight pricing data but does not yet offer flight availability information. But it will tell you what month (or even what week within a month) would have the best price to specific destinations, based upon historical patterns.

Employment

Monster, HotJobs, CareerBuilder, Craigslist and national newspaper sites from such prominent classified publishers such the *New York Times* already allow job hunters to search within a geographic area and even to pinpoint jobs within a mile or two of home base. New competitor SimplyHired—which raised $13.5 million in April 2007 from MySpace's parent company, Fox Interactive Media—is powering the newly launched MySpace Jobs. The service is oriented to the MySpace demographic and lists summer jobs like lifeguards and camp counselors, as well as internships and retail positions at Gap and Abercrombie and Fitch.

IT Search

Krugle has as its vision to "answer the need for a single place to find relevant code and critical technical information." The company claims that developers spend 20 to 25 percent of their time looking for code and technical information. Unlike Google or Yahoo!, Krugle crawls source code, whether in open repositories or within source code control systems.

Shopping

Shopping comparison sites like Shopping.com and Pricegrabber.com are essentially vertical search engines. Mpire.com is a newcomer to the space that allows users to view the most recent selling prices of millions of items (using data from eBay) and then compare those prices with similar items selling on Overstock.com, eBay, Craigslist and Amazon. Mpire can also show a graph of prices over a 30-day time period, and plans to add social networking features such as allowing users to submit product reviews or send items to friends. Mysimon.com, one of the oldest and still quite popular shopping comparison sites, is a former CNET property now owned by CBS.

With a slightly different approach to consumer electronics, Retrevo .com, launched in August 2008, aims to help buyers and owners of high-tech gadgets and gear find relevant answers to everyday questions. The site is of interest because it uses two AI techniques called "clustering" and "classification," commonly employed in pattern recognition applications, to aid in product discovery.

Music

Pandora describes itself as "a music discovery service designed to help you find and enjoy music that you will love." Its database includes 400,000 songs by 20,000 artists. Pandora is powered by the Music Genome Project, which has comprehensively analyzed the musical characteristics in its collection and serves up music that is similar to what you tell the service you already like. Once Pandora knows your favorite songs or artists, it launches a streaming station to "explore that part of the musical universe." But don't look for any classical music— the Music Genome Project doesn't include any yet.

Real Estate

Trulia, a residential real estate search engine, has announced the release of TruliaMap, an Internet tool available free to real estate brokers and agents that allows them to showcase their listings through mapping technology that automatically maps up to 50 property listings on a website. Since rolling out the feature, Trulia reports that usage of online maps from click-through to listings has increased more than 400 percent.

Zillow uses Google's ad-sale model while RealEstateABC and PropertyShark.com have a subscription model. Zillow has real estate agents in a virtual tizzy, so they must be doing something right. Zillow is the first major test of Google's ad-sale model for vertical search and they'll soon have their value estimates on almost 65 million houses. Zillow has Google ads, Pictometry pictures through MSN and loan quotes through LendingTree (part of InterActive Corp [IAC], along with Ask.com), and it supplies home value estimates to Yahoo! too.

Other Up and Comers

The business-to-business vertical goWholesale.com is geared specifically for wholesale buyers looking for suppliers and business owners looking for business services.

Eurekster (www.eurekster.com) enables any publisher to create, manage and monetize vertical search for any subject or area where they have passion, expertise, content, advertisers, etc. Then the community/social data further refines the already highly specialized results. Eurekster currently powers vertical or social search for close to 20,000 publishers worldwide.

MOBILE SEARCH

Much is expected of mobile search. It is an area in which Google's dominance is not hegemonic and Yahoo! and several upstarts intend to give Google a run for its money.

However, Google has rolled out a new standard for search-enabled mobile phones that are just beginning to come to market. While GPS

functionality has been seen as a key to effective mobile search (allowing users to get geo-targeted results), Google technology allows geo-
targeting without GPS by triangulating cell phone signals. Expect
many developments in this area as search meets localized shopping,
not to mention fierce competition for listings among restaurants in this
space.

The development of mobile search alone is expected to be a boon
for local search, as local search will facilitate the ability for people to
not just find a business serving their need, but one that has a bricks-
and-mortar presence within driving or walking distance. Creating
web pages for mobile search is becoming easier: Google has a page
creator (www.pages.google.com) that works in XHTML, and independent developers such as www.winksite.com offer community
and support.

AFFILIATE SEARCH

Bob had the opportunity to attend the Affiliate Summit in Las Vegas
recently and was reminded once again that some of the savviest search
marketers are that group of affiliate marketers generally known as
"search affiliates."

While "content affiliates" attract audiences by offering a deep level
of subject information before directing buyers to merchant pages,
"search affiliates" buy keywords and live on the arbitrage between the
click cost and the affiliate sale payment on conversions.

In this group can be found some of the most knowledgeable search
marketers on the web. They live search 24/7. They depend on their SEM
prowess to pay the mortgage or their kid's school tuition.

There is a current controversy in the affiliate world as to the proper
relationship between the search affiliates and the merchants for whom
they are a channel. The trend is for merchants to increasingly limit the

affiliates on what brand- and product-related keywords they can bid on or how high they can bid. This is to minimize potential bid competition between merchant and affiliate.

Some search affiliates maintain that this is a short-sighted policy and point out that, in the search affiliate model, it is the affiliates who are, in effect, financing the merchants' search marketing budget. Many merchants counter that the search affiliates "cannibalize" sales that should go directly to them. Advocates for the search affiliates maintain that they can be responsible for 10 to 30 percent of merchants' affiliate program sales, and that they provide the opportunity for merchants to gain traffic from multiple ads appearing on a search results page.

Some "search affiliates" may not even have a website, only a referring URL. While the search engines have rules about display URLs being the same as destination URLs, these rules are not always being followed. The number of rogue affiliates is probably low, but the issue is worrisome for merchants.

Of course, with Yahoo! having implemented Panama, all the leading search engines are now opaque when it comes to discerning the bid landscape. As a result, merchants can't see what their affiliates are bidding. This makes enforcement of merchant bidding restrictions somewhat problematical and increases the pressure for merchants to totally ban affiliate competitive keyword bidding, especially on brand words.

However this controversy plays out, it's always worth paying attention to what the search affiliates are doing. You're probably bidding against them.

VIDEO SEARCH

The video search function of Google has been around a while, though it is fairly hidden under the "more" tab on the menu bar, but it can be used to return video results to a search query. MSN has video search as do most of the news destination sites. Video search and video search advertising are more easily optimized if you understand online video in depth, so we're giving that its own chapter, Chapter 6. However, we do want to mention some other important and emerging players in the web video search arena that have quickly earned their stripes.

Blinkx (www.blinkx.com) is a category leader in dedicated video search, with over 18 million video clips collected from news, sports, entertainment and personal web outlets. It indexes video clips from around the web and allow users to search them on Blinkx.com and partner sites. The Blinkx technology combines voice recognition with image and contextual analysis. The company has a partnership with Microsoft to power the video search on MSN and Live.com. Blinkx claims the deal made it the "single biggest video search engine on the Web." Blinkx already powers video search on AOL, Lycos, Times Online and other major sites.

Other competitors:

Flurl (www.flurl.com) is a Belgium-based video search firm in which Brad Greenspan, the founder of MySpace, has acquired a majority stake. Flurl claims to be the "leading independent video search engine." In addition to video, Flurl also indexes images and audio and flash content.

PureVideo (www.purevideo.com) is a video search engine that enables users to search within the most popular video directories and video-sharing sites. It also provides a celebrity video directory. Every search result has its own RSS feed, and you can track its status through any feed readers.

Users of Pixsy (www.pixsy.com) can search across dozens of video sites and can save searches and single videos to watch again. Pixsy displays a description of the content of each video, when available, and enables emailing search results. The company is a B-to-B provider and powers search for many entertainment and corporate sites.

Truveo (www.truveo.com) is a unit of AOL that offers cross-platform video search and also powers many large sites.

Expect a lot of consolidation in this area as larger firms acquire budding technologies, and start-ups continue to emerge.

LET'S GO VIRAL

Creating Buzz

A brand is what a friend tells a friend it is. Not what a company tells them.

—SCOTT COOK, FOUNDER OF INTUIT

MARKETING WITHIN SOCIAL NETWORKS—such as MySpace, file-sharing sites like Flickr, and personal search pages such as Yahoo! Answers—is best approached from a PR perspective, and not as an online ad buy. Why? One reason is that social networks, like virtual worlds, are often hostile to hard sell messages. According to eMarketer, $920 million was spent by advertisers on social networks. A lot of it went to branded entertainment and a lot of it didn't work. "Softer" promotions, such as contests and sponsored entertainment, have proven to be successful, but like event marketing in the real world, these need word of mouth to succeed. From a marketer's perspective, a better reason is that it is often possible to create successful buzz within a social network, with just a shoestring budget and a widget or two.

"Word of Web" Marketing:
The Basics

We've all heard about word of mouth as a driver for business success for a long time. It has been considered, like PR, to be "poor man's marketing" because companies with no real marketing budget often rely heavily on word of mouth. When lecturing for classes, Leland has found that many students, when not sure about how they will market a product contemplated in an assignment, will simply say "word of mouth."

On the web, word of mouth no longer is an ethereal concept. "Word of web" is a proven best practice to promote your product or your organization's mission. There is no longer the need to just hope that your product or service will be talked about due to some cosmic alignment of the stars. Online marketers are savvy in how to tap into the power of word of web, and are developing methodologies by which to improve and measure its effectiveness.

A key tenet of word of web marketing is empowerment. You must empower your customer to share his or her experience and engage them fully in the exchange, to help you achieve your marketing objective. To do this, you must let go of the message to a certain extent. This can be frightening to a traditional-thinking enterprise. But, you must do this—and perhaps take comfort in the fact that allowing peer advocates to do the talking for you is ridiculously less expensive than any paid media campaign, and, if managed properly, is seriously more effective.

Andy Sernovitz, former CEO of the Word of Mouth Marketing Association and author of *Word of Mouth Marketing: How Smart Companies Get People Talking* (New York: Kaplan Business, 2006, www.wordofmouthbook.com) breaks word of mouth into five "T" steps: talkers, topic, tools, take part, and track.

1. *Find the Talkers: Locate people likely to relay your word of mouth message.* Talkers are often referred to as "influentials," but they can be any group of people who have the enthusiasm and connections to relay your message to the target audience. They may be part of a formal evangelism program, or they can be bloggers who happen to cover your topic. Sometimes they are new customers bubbling with enthusiasm; sometimes rabid fans willing to spread your message.

Learn to identify the right core group and give them a topic that they are willing to talk about.

2. *Select Topics: Choose portable concepts that are simple ideas to share.* All word of mouth centers on creating the message that you want to spread. Good topics are portable: simple ideas that one person can relay to another. They can be sophisticated brand-building concepts, something as simple as a special discount coupon or a tangential idea like "JetBlue has TVs."

The specifics of the message don't matter, but you need to give people something, a clear, simple idea that can be relayed successfully.

Find a topic that is interesting enough to motivate your talkers, then give them tools to help facilitate that conversation.

3. *Get Tools: Technology makes it easier for word of mouth to take place.* Word of mouth (WOM) marketers make their biggest impact when they *provide the infrastructure* to help messages spread. Word of mouth as a marketing technique is largely due to the growth of the tools that we have to support WOM conversations. A special friends-and-family discount may be worth talking about, but it has exponentially more marketing power when you pack it into an easy-to-forward email. A blog is a tool that enables a company to talk directly with fans, and so is viral video likely to be "mashed up"—sliced and diced for the amusement of the web masses.

Keep these and all positive conversation going by taking a larger part in it.

4. *Take Part: Participate and engage in a genuine two-way dialogue.* This is the hardest part for most marketers to work with. When you open the door to real people, and encourage them to start talking about your brand, they expect you to participate in that conversation. You need to respond to their messages, you need to accept comments on your blog, you need to participate in giving them a story to share. Online communities create a home and focus for otherwise disparate conversations. Formal evangelism programs provide the support and encouragement that keeps fans talking.

Once you open the door to word of mouth conversations with your talkers, there is no way to shut it again. You'll get negative feedback, you'll get crackpots, and you'll need to assign staff to listen and learn from the conversation. At the same time, however, you'll be earning the respect and recommendation of your customers and building powerful long-term relationships.

Track the conversation and build it into your marketing plan.

5. *Tracking: Measure the online conversation.* Amazing tools have been developed in the past two years that enable us to understand how word of mouth conversations travel and how we can follow what consumers are saying about companies. The rapid growth of blogs and online communities have put much of the verbal consumer-to-consumer conversations in writing, and when it's written down it's much easier to measure. From there, we can take that online conversation and project it into the offline world.

This represents a major knowledge boom for marketers. It lets you understand what consumers really think about your brand, your marketing and your products. It provides a level of genuine understanding that is more authentic than the data squeezed out of focus groups.

Learn to value raw consumer feedback and to use it to build better companies.

A NEW METRIC? WOMS!

Conversations about your products and services matter. Services like Nielsen's Buzz Metrics (www.nielsenbuzzmetrics.com) monitor the blogosphere to measure product mentions. Some are even starting to categorize conversations as "WOM units," or "WOMs." Think like an advertising executive for a moment. In advertising everything is measured: the number of times a commercial appears, the number of times an ad runs in the newspaper or in a magazine, etc. Those frequencies are then compared to movement in the sales needle (hopefully an uptick!). With a WOM unit, the number of times a brand or a product is mentioned online in blog conversations is measured, and the effect of those conversations on sales volume is calculated.

When you think about how much credence most people give the recommendation of a friend in a purchasing decision, you begin to understand its power. Nielsen surveys indicate that consumers trust recommendations from other consumers more than any other form of advertising, and there's plenty of evidence backing them up. A study released by the American Management Association surveyed 1,174 people online and found that 22 percent said they would read or write a product review on a blog, 45 percent said they would visit a social networking site to find information on sales and discounts, and 47 percent said they would go to a social networking site to download coupons or get ideas for holiday gifts.

SOCIAL NETWORKS: YOUR NEW BEST FRIEND

Online communities date back to the earliest days of the Internet—the 1970s when government researchers and academicians would share results and debate outcomes on Usenet. This was long before the World Wide Web or graphical user interfaces made interacting with others online a user-friendly experience.

Figure 5-1 Pass-alongs can be simple and effective

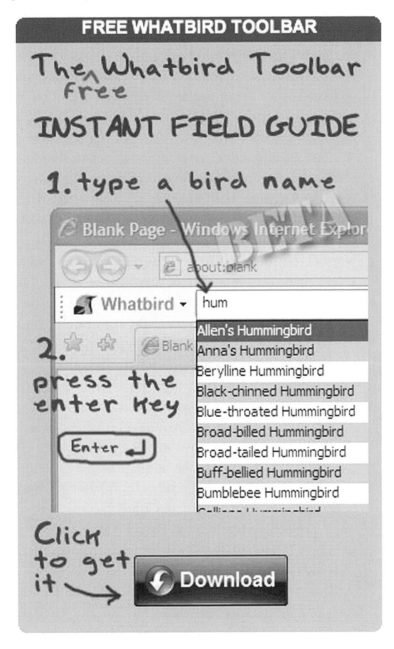

The Internet has made it easy for vast communities of people with specific niche interests to find one another and share their passions with one another. The auction site eBay was created by Pierre Omidyar so that his fiancée would have a place to buy and sell the Pez dispensers she collected. A community of Pez enthusiasts came together, which spawned other communities of collectors, and the world's largest marketplace was born. The pixie dust that made this so magical was people connecting with people who shared their passions.

Past attempts to create communities online have ranged from the successful entrepreneur (dogster.com, mediabistro.com, chow.com) to corporate giants, including iVillage.com (NBC Universal) and Being-Girl.com, a site for teens from Procter & Gamble. As the most successful communities are those that grow organically by word of web and word of mouth, creating your own community from scratch takes considerable resources and may take years to catch fire. Piggybacking on an established network, either as an advertising sponsor or as a stealth contributor feeding messages to the community, is cheaper and quicker.

Social networks are available for groups from cradle to grave. Disney offers Club Penguin (www.clubpenguin.com) for the youngsters, and Eons (www.eons.com) is geared toward the 55 and older set. In between you have MySpace (www.myspace.com) and Facebook (www.facebook.com) as the two largest, and LinkedIn (www.linkedin.com) for the business set. You have social bookmarking sites like Del.icio.us (www.del.icio.us), social scheduling sites like Zvent (www.zvent.com) and Upcoming (www.upcoming.yahoo.com), social sharing sites like Flickr (www.flickr.com) for photos and YouTube (www.youtube.com) for videos, social project management in Basecamp (www.basecamphq.com), social search in Yahoo! Answers (www.answers.yahoo.com) and social ranking with digg (www.digg.com).

Even more narrowly formed communities include lifestyle networks such as Snooth (wine enthusiasts), Don'tStayIn (clubbing in the United Kingdom) and Divorce360 (recent divorce). This only scrapes the surface. Countless social applications and communities emerge on the web

Figure 5-2 Example of a file-sharing site

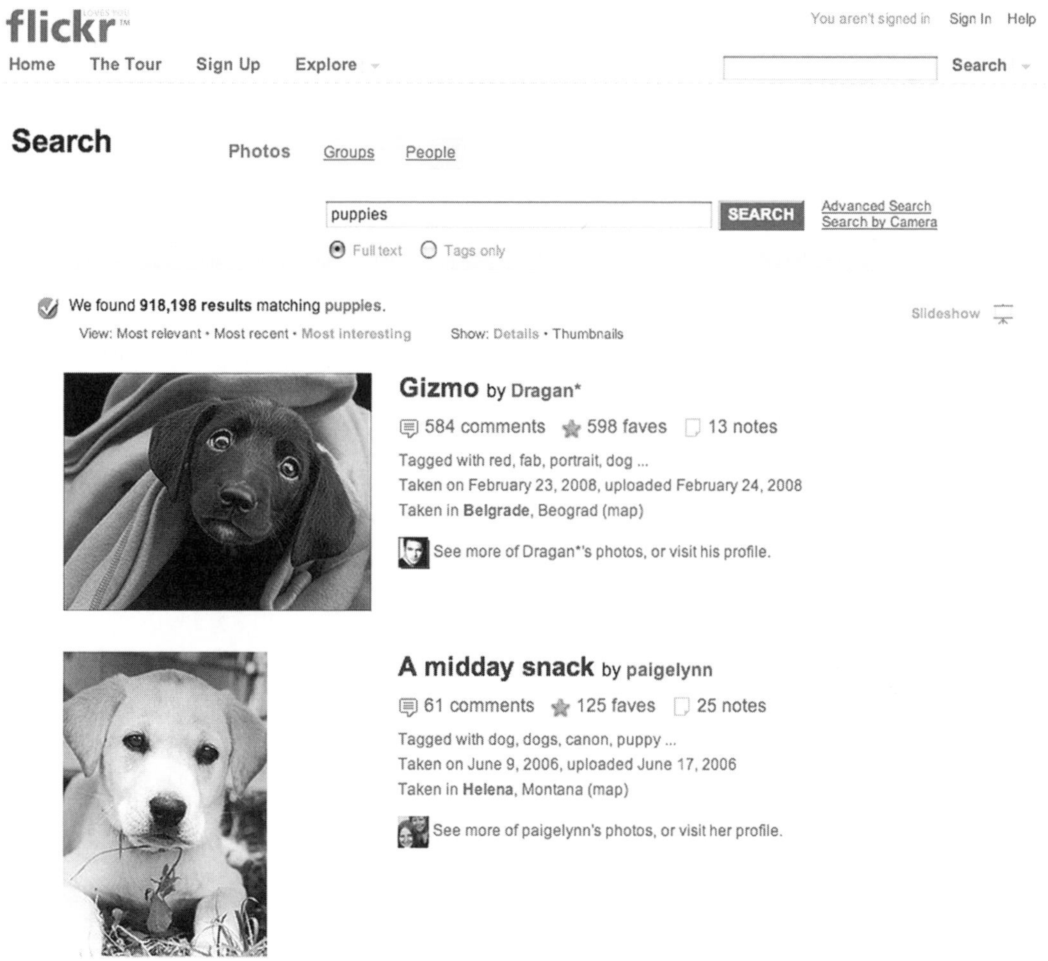

daily. If you want to try to predict the next hot thing, you could spend days watching the "what's hot" sections on www.ThisNext.com to see what people are buying.

To stay abreast of all of the news relating to social networks, there is no better source than Mashable (www.mashable.com).

As an online communications professional, you need to work in the social networks to create conversation with and connections to your brand. You can do this in several ways:

- Establish pages and groups for your brand on the social networks for your customers to connect with and join.

- Utilize the same research and engagement techniques we outline in Chapter 7 for connecting with bloggers. *Especially* the part about lurking and sitting on your hands for a while, while you get the mood and the tone of the community.

- Build widgets or other applications to sit on your social network page that your target audience will find useful and interesting and want to put on their pages. Then work to get adoption among your audience. You want your widget to be unique or interesting enough that users will place it on their pages, then their friends will do the same, etc. You want your widgets to go viral.

TARGETED MARKETING WITHIN SOCIAL NETWORKS

On the social networks, your customers become your "friend." When your customers join you, or become linked with your page on the social nets, *friend* becomes a verb, because they will "friend" you. This means that any time they update their profile or add something to their page, you will get notified of this. Conversely, any time you update the profile or add something of interest to your corporate page, everyone who has friended you will get notified. You can have special online events to which your friends are invited. You can give your friends special discount codes to be used on your e-commerce site. You can give your friends coupons. You can have contests for tickets to events your friends would find interesting. You will be directly connected to your customers and they to you. As you can see, if your friend network becomes large enough, you can move the sales needle for your company.

You'll also discover that some friends can be more important than others. Social networks spawn their own celebrities. One of the earliest examples of this can be found in 2006, when Unilever retained MySpace celebrity Christine Dolce, whose handle is ForBiddeN, to help them promote their Axe deodorant. This buxom bleached blonde boasted a friend network of more than 900,000 at the time. Tay Zonday, an amateur musician, caught the attention of Dr. Pepper with his YouTube video of a song he wrote called "Chocolate Rain." The video had millions of views and was well on its way to being a YouTube sensation. Dr. Pepper produced a professional video with Tay, recasting his song as "Cherry Chocolate Rain" to promote its new flavor, Cherry Chocolate Dr. Pepper. With the press attention this move garnered, and with the millions of views the new video has received on YouTube, there's no doubt that this collaboration was worth its weight in Cherry Chocolate Dr. Pepper.

Another key aspect of the Dr. Pepper campaign was that the online version did not parallel the new product launch in print media to its legacy (i.e., older) customers. Online can effectively segment customers and corrals new ones previously oblivious. WPP Group's Olgivy & Mather's online campaign for Dove cost a mere $150,000—a fraction of the spending it does for client Unilever—and was based around a viral video clip that showed an average-looking woman transformed into a supermodel by judicious use of airbrushing. "No wonder our perception of beauty is distorted" was the tag line. Posted on YouTube for digital file sharing, the video clip was viewed more than 24 million times on YouTube in its first year, and drew about 5 million views on the campaign website (www.campaignfor realbeauty.com).

Clearly this was not a campaign that would play in Unilever's traditional media: TV and women's home and fashion magazines. Yet it complemented the product's broader-reaching, overall campaign, which revolved around using non-models in advertisements in print and TV. More to the point, those 5 million views on the campaign website were from consumers intentionally interacting with the Dove brand. They became *engaged* consumers.

EXAMPLE: TARGET VS. WALMART ON MYSPACE

Approximately half of MySpace members are estimated to be college students. In 2007, both Target and Wal-Mart aimed their back-to-school promotions at this same market, and on the same theme: decorating your dormitory at school.

Target's approach, with a MySpace page design "Dorm Survival Guide" by agency AKQA, was to provide an information "environment" that included design advice, discussions, quirky takes on dorm food and a quiz that matched the furnishings selected with personality traits. Members were encouraged to upload and swap photos of how they had decorated their dorms, and also to comment on what they saw. Branding was limited to the bull's-eye logo and a banner that indicated the Target was the sponsor of the site. No ads ran on the site, but banner ads for Target that did run on Facebook linked only to the Facebook site, not to the retail website. By the end of the promotion, which ran from July to the end of September, the site drew 7,176 participants and hosted 37 discussion groups; in addition, more than 400 photos and 400 postings had been shared among the community.

Wal-Mart's version, "Roommate Style Match" was created by its primary agency Edelman and ran from August through October. While the concepts were similar, Wal-Mart's was built around a design quiz and similar interactive tools that visitors could use individually, but not together. It offered no discussion groups, but had a bulletin board, "The Wall," for comments. More than half of the early comments were critical of Wal-Mart's business policies. While this may have been anticipated (the company has many detractors online), the negative vibe was pervasive. Bravely, Wal-Mart kept the comments section running but couldn't stanch the flood. Bloggers weighed in and added more brickbats to The Wall. At the end of the promotion, approximately 2,000 participants had visited the site.

August is the prime month for back-to-school shopping in retail. According to the National Retail Federation, August 2007 overall sales were up by 3 percent over August 2006 at Wal-Mart. At Target, overall sales were up by 6 percent.

As the students might say, you do the math.

THE NEW WIDGET ECONOMY

Social network technology today makes it easier than ever for people with common interests to come together and stay connected. The largest social networks, Facebook and MySpace, view themselves as social *platforms* from which other applications for connecting can be launched. Facebook was the first to open up its code base so that others could append applications to their platform. MySpace soon followed suit. With the community adding and proliferating applications to serve itself, the social platforms become self-perpetuating, almost organic.

These platform appendages are movie quizzes, compatibility tests, social calendars, games, sports scores, news, recipes, jokes, Bible verses, book or white paper excerpts and many other embodiments of human interests. They are called widgets.

WIDGETS ARE SOCIAL CURRENCY

Widgets are not new but their applications to marketing are fairly recent. These self-contained packets of code that sit on top of web pages are designed so that users can create shortcuts or customize their web experience. In social networks, they create new ways of connecting. Network users up their status by discovering a widget first, posting it on their site and offering it to "friends" to borrow. If you provide a widget to your audience, you're giving them another method to pass around or republish your material. Since a widget is basically a shortcut window to content that exists and is maintained on your own web page, dissemination is automated and fairly trouble-free—and to a large extent, more controllable than other forms of word of web.

A host of consumer product brands have experimented with widgets, including Hewlett-Packard, Sony, Hallmark and Levi's, with varying levels of success. Widgets have applications to the business-to-business community if they can provide something more than entertainment.

Figure 5-3 An employment widget for the publishing community

The widget must provide something of value, and this can be as simple as a frequently updated data stream on a specific topic that rank-and-file employees might truly enjoy passing to their peer networks.

If you choose to add widgets to your social network arsenal, there are any number of developers on the web who will create them for you. To discover the most popular widgets currently on the social networks for business-to-business applications, go to www.widgetbox.com for a sampling. If you want more anecdotal information, doing a search for "best widgets" on any of the search engines will provide you with good information.

Widgets come in every shape and size. The cool factor can sometimes gain the most initial enthusiasm, but cool eventually becomes tepid. Think about what will be relevant and useful to your core audience. Again, this might not be directly product related, but it should be directly related to a need or aspiration of your community, and by branding your widget, you'll still gain the benefit. Your widget could help tie your audience in more tightly with your celebrity spokesperson. If your audience is ga-ga over a particular television show, do a deal with the producers and give them a widget with insider information. Newsfeeds, polls, compatibility tests, games, music, popularity contests, premier content—the possibilities for custom widgets are endless.

As long as you remember that social media is about building relationships and creating conversation with your community, sharing and not selling, and you play by the rules of the community, you will be effective with widget sharing.

VIRAL VIDEO

Video content can be repurposed in many formats: it can run on broadcast, then be on-demand on the web, and on-demand on Smartphones. Super Bowl ads, for example, take on a life of their own online.

The most popular downloadables today are video clips, a revolution made possible by the widespread reach of high-speed broadband carriers that can deliver an entire feature film to your home computer in a minute or two. The capability of cell phones to not only download and view, but share and transmit video clips wirelessly opens another door for messaging.

A young Stanford graduate student named Dan Ackerman Greenberg stirred up a tempest of controversy with an article he posted on *Tech Crunch,* an influential Silicon Valley blog. In the article, Dan identified the "secret strategies" behind many viral videos. Some of those secret strategies struck blog readers as deceptive, sparking a torrent of replies—over 500 comments, most of them bashing Dan. He responded with a second post, in which he disclaimed actually utilizing the most egregious techniques, but the controversy continued to swirl. We think Dan did everyone a favor by lifting the curtain on how videos can be manipulated. Our own strategies favor the creative use of paid media in addition to guerilla messaging to fuel virality. But it is well worth examining the techniques Dan identifies. Even if major brands and reputable agencies would eschew these practices, it is important to realize that you may be competing with other videos that are being promoted via dubious techniques.

Perhaps one of the most valuable lessons from Dan was a simple coding that allowed his clients to track their viral videos across the web. This was simply another code set ("?video=1") appended to the end of each URL, which made it faster to track inbound links using Google Analytics. TubeMogul and Vidmetrix (vidmetrix.com) were also used to track traffic around the web.

Dan sets as a goal 100,000 views. Below that he doesn't even charge. Among his claimed successes are six videos that achieved 6 million views on YouTube, with similarly high metrics for ratings, favorites, comments and links from blog posts.

Some of his tips seem obvious:

- Make it short.
- Don't make it an outright ad.
- Make it shocking.

Another tip is less obvious, but no less important:

- Design it for remixing.

This construct makes sense, since the value of a video clip improves if it can be shared in more innovative ways. So, rather than a dense information package, these viral shorts were made of simple components so that frames and frame sequences could be recombined by new artists.

But among the practices that stirred up controversy were:

- Use fake headlines.
- Appeal to sex.

Lost amid the controversy was some sound advice on how to get the vital first 50,000 views, which can rank up the viral message to Most Viewed of Day and Most Viewed of Week, by simply working your networks:

- Reach out to bloggers.
- Start forum threads and embed your video.
- Where allowed, embed your video in comments sections of MySpace pages.
- Share video with friends on Facebook.
- Send the video to an email list.

All these techniques can kick in during the vital first 48 hours when a video can move from Daily Most Viewed to Weekly Most Viewed, and they are equally applicable to a business-oriented message as they are to a consumer-targeted message.

Other techniques include title and thumbnail optimization. Titles of a viral video can be changed easily, so it is important to test and retest. The most striking image would ideally be the presentation thumbnail—the postage-stamp sized image that is a preview of the clip. Dan suggests changing out the thumbnail and using thumbnails that have a face or a person in it.

But Dan's critics focused on his recommendation of creating controversy by having "a conversation with yourself." In other words, stage a faux argument between multiple IDs that are all just you. Not that our old agency, Cybernautics, did not engage in such practices in online chat rooms on behalf of game clients back in Web 1.0 days, but most reputable markers have abandoned such practices. It's true, as Dan says, that "everyone loves a good heated discussion," but it is best practice not to fake one, if your ultimate goal is to establish authenticity and a good reputation in Web 2.0 communities.

CASE STUDY: **Sega: Kick-Starting Virality with the Sega Rally Revo™**

Sega is a worldwide leader in interactive entertainment, developing video game software and consoles for the masses. For the North America release of Rally Revo, the latest installment in the Sega Rally video game series, Sega of America Inc. tapped Mediasmith to provide media strategy, planning and buying services. Mediasmith partnered with production company Mekanism to develop the official website for Rally Revo, as well as four comedy videos featuring the misadventures of fictional racing partners Tonya and Donya. Mediasmith was tasked with building awareness of the Rally Revo release and staging a viral effect of the promotional videos, with the goal of driving traffic to the game's website and away from competitor games, and converting target audience members into Rally Revo gamers.

The challenge was influencing virality of the promotional videos and creating a buzz surrounding the product release, while not blatantly appearing as an advertiser, which would disrupt the domino effect characteristic of a viral video. Success would be measured by targeted reach and exposure, gamer buzz traffic, and the campaign's efficiency at driving traffic to the Rally Revo landing page.

Online Media Strategy

Mekanism developed a series of four short videos featuring Tonya and Donya, sequential in plot, with a new release every two weeks. Media efforts would promote the pilot video, while distribution of the remaining videos would rely solely on word of web, or buzz. Mediasmith's online strategy was to focus on sites that were gaming-centric and appropriate to the target audience. Mediasmith employed the use of video distribution products to pump up the number of video views on selected syndication sites and executed a high share of related voice ad placements. Ad placements included home page video sponsorship units, video "recommendations" and "editorial plugs" that distinguished Sega from other brand marketers on the page.

Results showed great success in influencing the viral effect. The Tonya and Donya pilot video received 17 times more views than would have been typical of such a video, as a result of high impact or editorial plug placements, which mixed in with editorial content seamlessly. In fact, editorial plug placements overdelivered by 100 percent, becoming the most efficient placement type for such an execution. Overall, 75 percent of the video views for the viral campaign were due to strategic media buys. Mediasmith's Elliot Kent-Uritam points out that this campaign shows that there is an alternative to simply trusting video virality to luck or creativity: you can enable virality more easily when you put media dollars behind it.

WEB VIDEO

The New, New Thing

WHY IS WEB VIDEO important?

There were 106 million users of Internet broadband in 2007: 74 percent of broadband users downloaded or watched online video. And, according to comScore, Inc., in the month of March 2008, more than 11 billion video clips were viewed online. The speed of adoption took everyone by surprise and it is estimated that 120 million Americans now watch a video online at least once a month. Heavy users of the medium watch a video online every day, and an estimated 65,000 clips are uploaded daily on YouTube, a popular video-sharing site.

How to describe this audience? According to a Pew Internet Life Study in 2007:

- 18–29 year olds are the most voracious video viewers.

- 27 percent of online video viewers watch news at least once a week.

- 26 percent watch funny videos once a week.

- 66 percent watch video ads and 46% take action on what they've seen.

- 76 percent tell a friend about a video they've seen.

Web video is exploding. Money is being invested in video search, video sharing, video advertising solutions and ways to measure all this activity. How these ventures will monetize video traffic is still unclear, but one of the most interesting developments in web video is its adoption by business-to-business companies who find the technology can provide compelling visuals to accompany product specs and promotions. With 15 percent of all Google searches done through the images tab, global search is becoming ever more visual, and a move to create

Figure 6-1 What America watches online

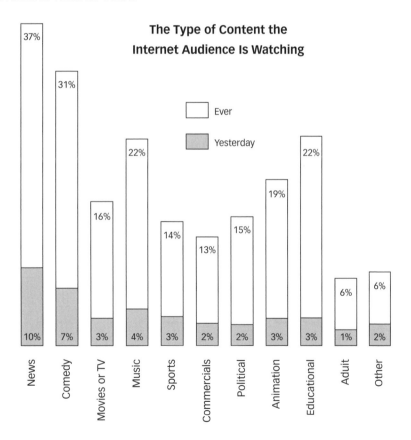

Figure 6-2 Where America watches video online

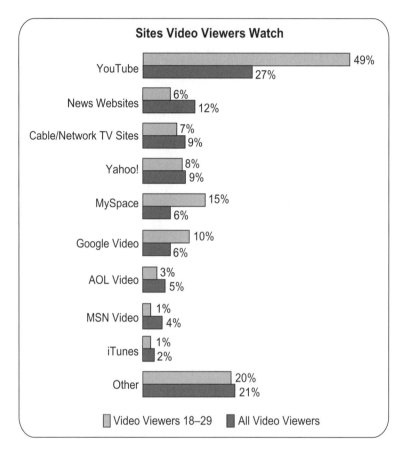

videos for your product, and then place them effectively, might offer the advantage you need against competitors.

INCOMING: WEBISODES AND ONLINE NETWORKS

Here are a few places where professionally created video content is available. If you're fired up and ready to approach this opportunity, here are some web sites to check out first. Ad-supported and broadcast industry–supported sites include:

- *iTunes*—iTunes (www.itunes.com), Apple's famous music site, is also one of the largest video download sites. Along with music, iTunes presents over 100,000 podcast video downloads. These include videos from independent creators as well as big names like HBO, NPR, ESPN, *The Onion,* CBS Sports and the *New York Times.*

- *Veoh.com*—Veoh is an independent Internet television broadcasting system that uses the Internet and peer-to-peer distribution. Ex-Disney chieftain Michael Eisner is an investor. Veoh consists of two main elements, the Veoh.com site, where you can browse the videos available on Veoh, create a user account and profile, interact with other broadcasters and viewers and preview videos within your browser. The second part of Veoh is VeohTV or its Veoh Player software application, which provides automatic delivery of full-length content for viewing on your PC (online or offline), or on your TV through a Flash interface.

- *Hulu.com*—A joint venture of Fox/News Corp and Universal, Hulu.com is still in the Beta stage as we write this. At Hulu, you will find programming across all genres and content types including TV shows, movies and clips, including current prime-time shows.

- *Revision3.com*—Imagined as a TV network for the web, creating and producing its own original, broadcast-quality shows, Revision3 has attracted a wide range of top advertisers including Sony, Netflix, Dolby, Microsoft, IBM, HP, Southern Comfort, Virgin America, Verizon and FX Networks.

Other companies like Next New Networks, Liquid Generation and many others are creating online video content series. Next New Networks is producing highly targeted content, such as Bride-o-rama.com, a video program network that delivers real advice from the recently married, and PulpSecret.com, dedicated to comic book news and culture. Liquidgeneration is heavily ad-supported and targets men between the ages of 18 and 24.

PEER-TO-PEER VIDEO-SHARING SITES (OR, BEYOND YOUTUBE)

BitTorrent (www.BitTorrent.com) is the technology behind much of the current peer-to-peer sharing on the Internet. While BitTorrent is not itself a network, it allows small Internet networks to be created to share files. BitTorrent is a prime example of an open network; anything added to the network can be copied and added to another network.

Enabling Technologies and Platforms

These new tools and suppliers include many set up for business use:

- *Brightcove* (www.brightcove.com) is a web video platform that serves clients like Discovery cable network, Dupont, and CBS. As with Veoh, users can place content into Brightcove via either the web or a desktop program. There are customizable video player templates and tools to distribute clips on blogs and on other sites.
- *Extend Media* (www.extend.com) concentrates primarily on creating Web video storefronts, where users can buy content. Customers include Showtime Networks, AT&T and Wal-Mart.
- *Magnify.net* (www.magnify.net) targets the smaller fish: niches, communities and enthusiast groups. In an interesting twist on the syndicated television models of old, Magnify.net's offering is free, with clients given 50 percent of all the page inventory on their

Magnify.net site to sell via their own ad networks or a Google AdSense account.

- *Maven Networks* (www.maven.net) provided ad-supported video platforms for major media companies like Fox News, Scripps Networks, Hearst and TV Guide. The tools allow clients to create playlists and build players, including a home-page player and smaller players for additional pages. In February 2008, this company was acquired by Yahoo!.

- *Multicast Media Technologies* (www.multicastmedia.com) understands the B-to-B marketplace, and provides video support to small- to medium-sized businesses. Clients include Realtor.com, Baby Universe, The Knot (a wedding site), Autotrader.com and others.

- *Narrowstep* (www.narrowstep.com) caters to international telecommunication companies such as Telefonica, Virgin Media and Telewest; it has also done work for Land Rover and other auto clients. Narrowstep offers embedded video players, standard template players and customized players. Monetization features include geographic targeting of ads, digital rights management, subscription models, pay-per-view, download-to-own, download-to-rent and sponsorship

- *Permission TV*'s expertise (www.permissiontv.com) is in creating interactive video experiences with social media and community features such as comment functions. Clients include Bob Vila's home improvement site and the Boston Symphony.

- *The Platform* (www.theplatform.com) is owned by Comcast, known for its expertise in cable narrowcast properties. It provides tools to integrate with other technologies. The Platform takes in content, manages the files, formats them into Quicktime, Flash, Windows or other formats and manages the metadata. The Platform also integrates with content delivery networks to publish files to other sites. Customers include NBC

Universal–News Corp's Hulu, BBC, CNBC, CBS's College Sports TV, Comcast and Hearst.

- *Roo* (www.rootv.com) is both an online TV platform and an aggregator of video from publishers such as Reuters, NYPost.com and Fox Television stations. A feature of Roo's distribution strategy is the use of peer-to-peer technology . . . because it owns a peer-to-peer network.

- *Twistage* (www.twistage.com) operates behind the scenes as a white-label online video provider: they'll provide the technology, the branding is all yours. The company powers web video for a variety of sites and offers the software, video player and other tools to load video onto the web.

- *WhiteBlox* (www.whiteblox.com) has provided turnkey solutions, services and support for a range of companies including nonprofits.

CONSUMER–CENTRIC VIDEO–SHARING SITES

YouTube is the largest of the video sharing sites but there are many, many YouTube competitors:

Consumer Sites Active in Video File Sharing

Altavista.com	Google Video	OpenVlog	SearchVideo.com
AOL Video	Grouper	Pixsy.com	Truveo
Blinkx.tv	Ifilm	Purevideo.com	TVGuide
Blip.tv	iKlipz	Putfile	Veoh
Dabble.com	JibJab	Revver	Yahoo! Video
Daily Motion	Lulu.com	Searchforvideo.com	YouTube
Flurl	MySpace		

ADVERTISING ON WEB VIDEO: A DIFFERENT ANIMAL

Unsurprisingly, online video viewers do not like ads placed at the beginning of clips, according to a Burst Media survey. Although the survey shows that more than half of all viewers will stop watching a video if it starts with an ad, viewers 18–24 years old tend to stay tuned.

Several forces come into play here: first, a great majority of early adoptors to the Internet are incredibly dismayed that advertising has come to the web. Second, late adoptors seem resigned to the fact that pop-ups and animated advertisements will appear as a hurdle to jump to get the content they crave. And, finally, a surprising number of current television advertisers expect to get along with TV ads as business as usual—which means we might well expect that any venture into online video advertising is likely to ape their broadcast efforts.

But, that would be a mistake.

Your initial experiment might be hiring an ad-serving company, such as DoubleClick, Atlas or Vindico. The value-add here is that such companies can guide you in standardizing the media elements in your campaigns, so you don't have to have your creative teams producing in a variety of formats rather than just one or two. Ad servers also provide a degree of third-party auditing of reach, page impressions and downloads, and can give you insights into video advertising networks that you may not be able to discover on your own.

If you're going solo, going with an ad network is another easy way to shorten the learning curve. National online video networks include Broadband Enterprises, Tremor Network and Roo. Services they provide include inventory search, as well as "blacklists"—used to protect your ad purchases by preventing similar ads by direct competitors from appearing on the same site.

BUYING WEB VIDEO: PRE-ROLLS, POST-ROLLS, MID-ROLLS, <u>PERSISTENT BANNERS</u>

The industry is in its infancy and there is little standardization of ad units. They range from pre-roll, to mid-roll, to post-roll, to pop-ups to companion banners. While there is much effort to repurpose 30-second TV spots, few users want to watch such lengthy ads. So there are experiments with shorter lengths such as 7 or 10 seconds. Whoever invents the online equivalent to TiVo's ad-skipping button will be able to retire in the Bahamas.

Ad pricing varies widely for popular Web shows, but can range from $15 to $20 per thousand views, according to Angela Gyetvan, VP of marketing and content at video-sharing site Revver (www.revver.com). The good news is that many outlets charge in pay-per-performance, and/or charge fees in line with quantifiable metrics such as page views. That means a show with 20,000 views at a $20 CPM (cost per thousand views) would cost about $400. This is a worthwhile experiment for many marketers.

"Ask a Ninja" is a web video show that reportedly generates around $1 million a year in advertising, licensing and merchandise. The Ask a Ninja team started the Web show in 2005 with an investment of about $60,000 from friends and family. Since then, they've generated 70 million views on YouTube, askaninja.com and other sites.

In mid-2006, deciding to try to maximize their web earnings, they partnered with video-sharing site Revver, which splits ad revenue 50–50 with content creators, and earned between $40,000 and $50,000 over an eight-month period.

Then they signed a seven-figure deal with Federated Media, which now sells ads for the show. In the last year, the number of "Ask a Ninja" views has increased from 2 million to 2.7 million per month. SanDisk, Palm, Doritos and Toshiba, among others, have signed up as sponsors. In Web 1.0, many pioneers crashed and burned trying to create original content for the web. Web 2.0 has made their visions reality.

But not everybody is as successful as the Ninja team. Dina Kaplan, COO at www.blip.tv, notes that it takes a lot of eyeballs to make a decent living. "Creators usually need at least 50,000 to 100,000 views per month before advertisers will take them seriously," she said.

"There is a very good chance that people creating shows that reach 500,000 viewers a month or more will be able to go full time," Ms. Kaplan said. "I don't know if you should quit your job, but if you reach 500,000 people a month or more, you will have opportunities to monetize it."

She advises that if a show has an audience of only 20,000 people per month, the creator should spend his or her time building an audience rather than finding a sponsor.

According to Ms. Kaplan, Blip.tv hosts a number of web series such as Rocketboom and Ze Frank, which attract those kinds of audiences.

AD-ENABLING TECHNOLOGIES AND VENDORS: A SHORT LIST

Here are some of the technologies and vendors providing helpful tools to web video advertisers:

- *ScanScout* (www.scanscout.com): ScanScout's technology creates new ad inventory alongside and within the video content time. It is designed to ensure that advertisers' brand messages will only be seen adjacent to the most appropriate content. In mid-2008 this company became an exclusive provider to Broadband Enterprises.

- *Broadband Enterprises* (www.broadbandenterprises.com): This revenue-sharing syndication company delivers a range of Internet ads from 150 advertisers to the over 2,000 sites in its network, and claims to support 20 percent of the total online video audience. In 2008 it began to produce original content.

- *YuMe* (www.yume.com): YuMe is a dedicated broadband video advertising network that can be delivered to any device—PC, TV, mobile and more—whether streamed or downloaded, with the ability to identify, classify and track content to ensure brand safety, contextual relevance, controlled syndication and consistent delivery across all digital media platforms—web, downloads, mobile and IPTV. YuMe Networks strikes deals with both advertisers and publishers to deliver ads across websites, mobile phones and peer-to-peer services. YuMe's ad formats include traditional ads such as pre- and post-roll, as well as interactive overlays, watermarks and menus.

- *Adap.tv* (www.adap.tv): This online video advertising service offers a OneSource platform that allows publishers and advertisers to match relevant advertising with online video content in fairly simple terms. The company uses advanced technology that adapts in real time to consumers' interests and their viewing behaviors. Adap starts with the premise that consumers don't like watching 15- or 30-second pre-roll ads before their online video. Instead, the company matches online video with short, contextual ads that appear as an overlay from publishers like Amazon, Yahoo! and LookSmart. A viewer can click on the ad to link to relevant products on Amazon, for instance.

- *Podaddies* (www.podaddies.com): Podaddies is a video advertising solution supported by its own video ad network, on a proprietary advertising platform.

- *Pluggd* (www.pluggd.tv; www.delvenetworks.com): Pluggd is of interest because it employs a search technology that combines speech recognition with semantic analysis of the video content. It then locates the portion of a video that best corresponds to a user's search and overlays a targeted ad, letting users jump to the exact section of the video they are most interested in.

ANALYSIS AND METRICS

We are turning over this section to people who are even more expert than we are—TubeMogul, an online video analytics company serving publishers large and small who need independent information about video performance on the web's top video sharing sites. TubeMugul also offers a free tool for posting videos to multiple websites that is being used by over 10,000 video creators.

The folks at TubeMogul.com have compiled a report titled, "Web Video Marketing—Best Practices," which they are allowing us to share with you. We think it is not only great advice for marketers wishing to maximize their ad dollars in web video, but correlative to similar practices to employ when attempting viral video distribution.

HERE'S THE PITCH: BEST PRACTICES FROM TEAM TUBEMOGUL

Online video is one of the best venues to engage an audience—don't even think about excluding it! This new medium allows the video creator to communicate a message on multiple levels—via visual imagery, the spoken word, music and visual text. It may sound like a commercial for a Montessori school—but this is the way people learn, and consequently, the way legendary brands are created. As a case in point, think of traditional Internet marketing; when was the last time that a paid search listing or banner ad raised your blood pressure or induced you to forward something to a friend? Get the point?

With online video you can also reach a huge audience for a minimal investment, thus the ROI of online video marketing can be astounding. Consider that according to the Interactive Advertising Bureau, more than 50 percent of the U.S. population will watch video online in 2008. That's 155.2 million people, and we're just talking the United States! Increasingly, people are watching a lot of video as well. According to comScore, Inc., Americans watched 9 billion online videos just in the month of July 2007, and by summer 2008 viewership had increased to nearly 12 billion videos—a more than 30 percent jump.

Like everything else, there is no "free lunch"—the video-sharing sites don't charge to host your content, but getting your target audience to watch and forward your video is no easy feat. That's where we come in. Since we are tracking videos across the major video-sharing and social networking sites, we know a thing or two about what works and what doesn't.

"Secret Formula": .5C + .15M + .20T + .15P = Success

Alright, we admit that an exact formula may be a bit oversimplistic, but when it comes to deciding how to allocate time and resources on a video intended to market something virally, the weighting of these four components should follow closely to something like this: That's it. Write down the formula above on a cocktail napkin and you have the code cracker for getting people to watch and forward your video. The formula above says that creating a video is a weighted function of four components:

> 50% C = Content and Production—this is storyline, style, lighting, production etc.
>
> 15% M = Metadata—the text title, keywords, descriptions, and categories that help people find your video
>
> 20% T = Thumbnail—the packaging that draws people in when displayed on the page
>
> 15% P = Promotion—just good old-fashioned marketing

These aspects help communicate your message far and wide in a way that makes an emotional connection with the viewers in a way that motivates them to pass it along to others. Now we will dive into each component of the secret video marketing formula.

Content and Production (.5C)

We know now that 50 percent of creating a great viral video is about content and production. The goal in this stage is to create something remarkable—literally, something that causes people to remark—and in doing so to effectively convey your message. We've noticed that certain categories tend to garner the interest of large audiences. Regardless of your message, utilizing a proven content category to package your message is a good way to spread your message wide and far. The remarkable comes in many shapes and sizes:

- Humor: everyone loves a laugh, but many of us like to make others laugh as well; this is what makes comedic videos so viral.
- Avant-garde videos: videos that push the boundaries of what is acceptable can be incredibly viral—especially since this content never makes it to network TV. But be careful not to damage your brand and to obey by the terms and conditions of the respective video-sharing sites.
- Talent: true talent is rare and fascinating. If you can showcase true talent, people will forward your video.
- Celebrities: we are fascinated with celebrities, and videos featuring a celebrity are very viral, in part because there are hundreds of websites that follow celebrities and will embed these videos. Beyond virality, celebrity endorsements have a powerful influence on decision making.
- Kitsch: don't kill the messenger, but a remarkable number of the most popular videos we are tracking also contain one or more of the following qualities:

  ○ Special effects: the Ray Ban sunglass catching video is a great example. In general, any video that generates debate generates viewers.
  ○ Animal/pet tricks: man is drawn to animals just as he is to fire . . . it's hard to explain, but it seems to have to do with primitive wiring in the brain.

- Cute kids: one of the draws of online video is that real people capture real moments, and nothing is as straightforward as a child just being herself.
- Repetitive, catchy music: certainly not a new concept, but with infinite channels come many more opportunities to put up the experimental jingle.
- Physical injury: thank goodness it's not me!
- Pranks: thank goodness it's not me!
- Spoofs: ride the coattails of the tried and true.
- And of course, sex always sells.

The trick, as with any marketing effort, is to both be remarkable *and* communicate your message. Use the right package to make your video a hit, but don't create a vehicle without passengers. Make sure the content is doing what it is supposed to do.

In the online video community, discussions around production are typically in reference to video quality—as it relates to camera, sound, compression, and editing. Some believe that higher production quality is an important component in gaining popularity for one's online videos, while others believe that the popularity of the medium is authenticity, and that lower quality video has a genuine nature that gets lost with higher quality. Given the plethora of widely seen videos over the Internet, this concept of quality hasn't seemed to correlate with audience size or popularity. One thing is for certain: high-quality human components of production, such as shooting and editing, make any video more watchable. Paying attention to lighting, framing the shot, and crisp editing is not only more pleasant, it's often required to make the picture viewable in a small window and on sites with file size restrictions.

Bottom line: choose production components that fit with your message, content, and intended audience.

Some great resources for tips on video production can be found at such sites as:

videomaker.com

reelseo.com

studio.metacafe.com (along with many of the sharing sites)

ourmedia.org/learning-center/video

www.theshirtlessapprentice.com

www.digitalvideosolutions.com

Metadata (.15M)

Each video-sharing site let's you create "tags," which are words that describe your video. These tags, along with the title and description of the video, are the basis for how your video is located by end users on video-sharing sites like YouTube. This is a simple concept, so it's remarkable that so many content creators screw it up.

Good use of metadata for video has recently become a requirement. Search engine optimization and search engine marketing used to be the realm of text only, but with search engines like Google and Ask adding video to their search results ("Universal" and "3-D" search, respectively), optimizing the metadata around your videos is increasingly important. This means creating rich and relevant video titles, descriptions and tags.

There are only a few specifics that you need to know about tags. First, max out the tags, title and description for every site. The more metadata describing your video, the more likely someone is to find your video. It's surprising to see so many uploaders let so much opportunity go to waste by adding few or nondescript tags. Second, your tags, and particularly the category you choose, should be relevant to your video. We have seen video creators go from little viewership to becoming regularly featured producers simply through a better choice of category.

If you are hosting a video on your own site, the same rules apply. But in such a case, be sure to create a relevant file name for your video. It is also advisable to have just one video per page with a simple text title and description place near the video itself. It's important to keep in mind that most videos are watched in social networking sites, blogs and content sites—not video-sharing sites. This means that while you may post your video to YouTube or MetaCafe, many of the views are a result of people embedding that video into another site. The implication is that your video should be hosted on both your website and the video-sharing sites for maximum exposure.

One more hint on tags—the TubeMogul "Load and Track" tool shows you how your tags will look on each site as you are uploading videos, and soon will show you the most popular tags and video search terms to help you select appropriate metadata.

Promotion (.15P)

Videos that have relevant and rich tags and descriptions will be found and will be forwarded. But there is nothing wrong with supercharging this process, and this is where promotion comes into play. This is especially important as many video sites employ a "bubble up" methodology that promotes videos and content creators, which receive the most views, subscribers, comments, ratings and forwards. These videos, then, "bubble up" to the top of video sites and become even more popular. So in the video world, popularity begets more popularity.

Building a community is the single best method for promoting a video. This isn't an overnight process, but can be done by using the infrastructure of the various video-sharing and social networking sites. This means subscribing to people's videos and leaving creative comments so that people click on your profile. Also, it's important (and fun) to befriend people and invite them to subscribe to your video channels. You can also join and be a meaningful contributor to various newsgroups and chat rooms. If you can pull off these things, you've just created your own set of groupies that will watch your content just because of the relationship, and this applies to both companies and individuals. Yet another way to build community is to write an interesting blog and create a following, as well as responding to the blog posts of others. Also, you'll be surprised how open bloggers and category experts will be to plug your video in exchange for a "sneak peak" or an interview.

Also consider submitting your videos to other Web 2.0 websites that employ voting systems to promote content. Some of the most popular sites are Digg, Reddit, Del.icio.us and StumbleUpon. As your video or article gains more votes, the video will attract even more attention and may even end up in a featured or top 10 category, which can generate hundreds of thousands of views in a day.

Generally, deploying videos to multiple sites makes sense as different sites have different content niches and audiences. Essentially, each site represents a community opportunity that you can tap into. TubeMogul "Load and Track" is an easy tool to deploy to multiple sites at once. Here is a handy grid that provides some information on a few of the top video-sharing sites:

Thumbnails (.20T)

The last component of our secret formula, and often the most overlooked, is the thumbnail. A thumbnail is the single image that represents your video. This is the image that someone will see before they decide whether or not to watch the video. If your thumbnail is bad it often doesn't matter if you got all of the other components of the formula right.

So what makes a good thumbnail? Typically thumbnails that are relevant and match the video title, description and tags are all you need. Beyond this, try to select the image that best captures the essence of your video. Unfortunately, each of the video-sharing sites has a different methodology for determining which frame will comprise the thumbnail. At one point, for example, YouTube used the frame that is in the very center of your video as the thumbnail, then they used 1:20 into the video, and now you have a choice of three frames. Other sites give you more options. It will pay off to invest the time to understand how the thumbnail is determined for every site where you deploy your video.

If you have any doubts about the power of thumbnails just check out this video on YouTube (youtube.com/watch?v=nhSZs-aAZb). The video features a thumb-

Figure 6-3 Cheat sheet on popular video-sharing sites

	Description	Demographics	Registration	Upload	Notes
YouTube	No intro needed here	Evenly female/male audience, even age distribution, U.S. East and West coasts.	Easy	Fast review process, mainly automated	Experimenting with and sharing
Yahoo! Video	An original video destination, but late to the game	Slightly more male viewers, slightly older, even U.S. geographic distribution	Medium	Relatively slow and unpredictable review process	
MySpace	Primarily a social networking site, but video is still huge	High percentage of female and under 18 viewers	Easy	New review process. Videos go live immediately	Being rebranded as MySpaceTV
Metacafe	Popular worldwide, prides itself on community votes driving featured content	Skews toward older, more educated, male viewers	Easy	Fast human review process	Offers and sharing
Google Video	Increasingly becoming more of a video search engine	Slightly more male viewers, disproportionately more Hispanic audience	Medium	Limited review process. Unlimited content length and size	Integrates with other Google apps like Web Albums and Picasa
Revver	One of the first video sites to offer ad revenue sharing	Slightly older, white male crowd	Easy	Discriminating human review process	Ads inserted into all videos
Daily-Motion	The YouTube of Europe	Overwhelmingly white male. Higher age and income than most	Easy	Fast and easy	Growing in the U.S.
Blip.tv	Publisher-friendly video sharing and distribution site	Slightly more male, slightly higher income level than most video sites, even ethnic distribution	Easy	Easy	Publisher can choose to insert ads
Brightcove	Trying to bring TV to the Internet	Even split male and female. Few under 18 viewers	Easy	Easy	Ad share options available
Crackle	Focused on making people stars	Largely male, disproportionately African-American audience	Easy	Slick Flash upload tool allows many videos in one shot	Owned by Sony
Veoh	Focused on full-screen video programming for anyone with a broadband connection	Slightly more male viewers, predominantly Asian, distributed across all age categories	Medium	Easy	Investors include Michael Eisner and Time Warner

[*Source:* TubeMogul]

nail of Britney Spears topless, but the viewer is soon disappointed to see that the video never delivers upon its promise. In fact, the video has no content, just two frames played over and over—this hasn't stopped close to 7 million people from watching the video!

There are thousands of successful commercial videos that have gone viral, but we thought we'd share with you a few of our favorites:

Nike's "Touch of Gold" (http://www.youtube.com/watch?v=lsO6D1rwrKc)

Figure 6-4 25 million views—quite a score

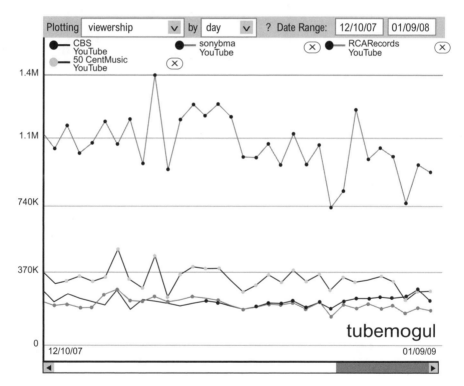

This video features Ronaldinho—one of the most famous footballers in the world. He is sitting on the practice field and all is quiet, when he is presented with a gold box containing a pair of gold Nikes. After putting on the shoes he goes on to hit the crossbar with a soccer ball four times without the ball ever hitting the ground. You find yourself wondering, "Did he really do that?" At the end, the URL nikefootball.com is displayed—the message comes across loud and clear. As of August 2008, this video has been viewed over 24 million times on YouTube alone and continues to garner around 30,000 views daily, even though it has a grainy quality.

Blendtec's "Will It Blend?" video series (www.willitblend.com).

Figure 6-5 Blendtec uses geeky humor to create interest

Think blenders can't be viral? Blendtec created a video show, complete with theme music and a host that feature their blenders pureeing everything from iPhones to Chuck Norris dolls. The videos are hilarious and definitely convey the message that Blendtec blenders are badass. While the videos are distributed on video-sharing sites, the company also built an entire website around the concept. In their first year of exposure the videos generated well over 30 million views! Think about what that would cost on network television.

FrenchMaidTV's "How To Register A Domain" (www.youtube.com/watch?v=dDwYnGQRPng).

Figure 6-6 Sex still sells, even in B-to-B

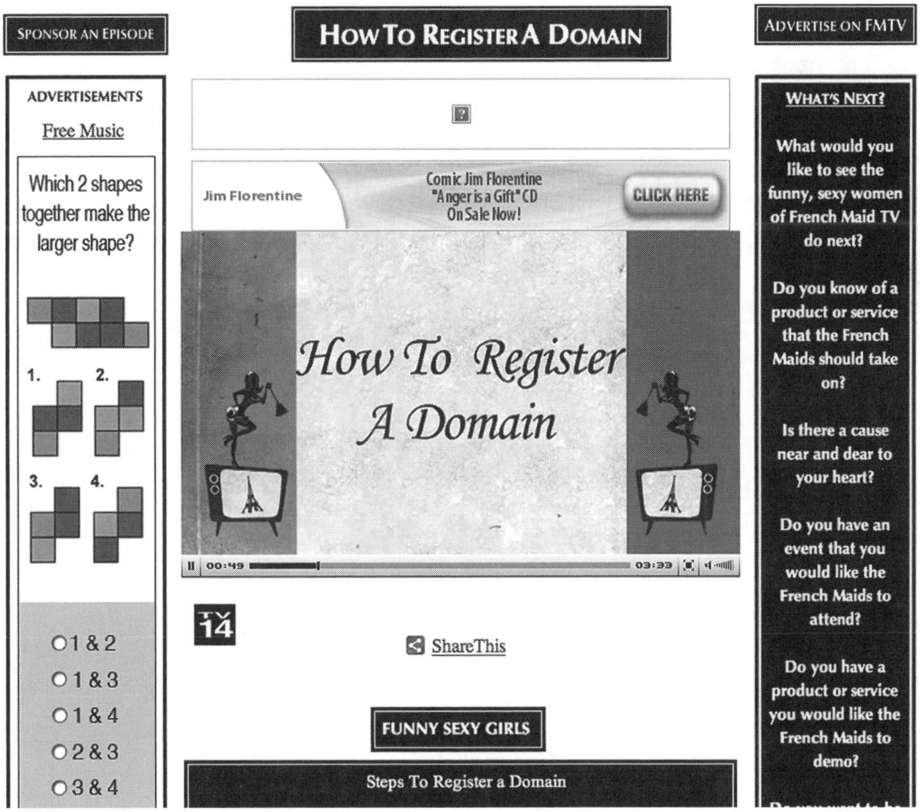

Think of the last trade show you attended—the most popular booth was probably the one seeded with scantily clad and beautiful women. Take that same concept, inject steroids, and you have FrenchMaidTV (www.frenchmaidtv.com), where sexy French maids demo products. In this video, the maids show us how to register a domain on GoDaddy. Beyond the obvious attraction, the videos are well produced and feature over the top humorous French accents and interesting storylines, reminiscent of an old Benny Hill comedy spoof.

Summary

Online video is a powerful medium for marketing because of its engagement potential, SEO value and measurement opportunities. There are specific steps you should take to maximize the chances of producing a wildly popular (and widely viewed) web video campaign, and specific tools to help manage those steps. Remember to choose content that is remarkable and incites an emotional connection with the viewer, recognize the value of both metadata (to help your videos get found) and thumbnails (to draw in viewers), and last, use the platforms at your disposal to build communities around your video messages. Online video is a powerful marketing tool if you use it to the fullest!

AFFILIATE MARKETING

The Automated Referral Network

BUSINESS-TO-BUSINESS WEBSITES often forget the value of web affiliate programs, which help improve your search rankings and can serve you well as a lead generator and community builder. Check your competitors' websites—do they offer an affiliate program? If they do, you should as well. If they don't—then you've got a tool you can use to some advantage.

In an online affiliate marketing program, a website owner receives a commission for generating a transaction, such as a lead or sale, or for facilitating a web visitor's travel by linking to the website of a merchant or an advertiser. The merchant provides the website owner with a visual logo or banners, encoded with URL links to the website and perhaps a particular "buy page" for a specific product. The website owner, often also referred to as a "publisher," provides some room, typically on the home page, topic page or a links page, to accommodate the artwork and links. When customers pass through to the merchant site, the merchant pays the website owner for facilitating the referral.

Affiliate programs are performance-based; the merchant pays a commission usually only when a transaction has occurred and can be verified to the satisfaction of both parties.

Amazon popularized the affiliate model, although it wasn't the first to use it. In November 1991, CDNow, a music site, launched its BuyWeb program, becoming the first nonporn site to offer a monetized affiliate or associate relationship rather than a simple, mutual free link from one site to another.

Starting in July 1996, if Amazon affiliates placed a banner or text links on their site for books or other products, users could go to Amazon, and if they bought something the affiliate website would get a commission check. Less than three years later, some 600,000 affiliates were receiving checks and many more are now sharing the wealth of an industry giant.

In February 2000, Amazon.com announced that it had been granted a patent (6,029,141) on all the essential components of an affiliate program. The patent application was submitted in June 1997.

Today, 80 percent of affiliate programs use cost per sale (CPS) as a compensation method and 19 percent use cost per action (CPA). The remaining 1 percent use other methods, such as cost per click (CPC) or cost per thousand (CPM)—and we suspect these are mostly merchants who haven't bothered to update their affiliate programs since they started them in the 1990s. This report was based on survey responses from almost 200 affiliate managers from a cross section of the industry.

Many large merchant sites maintain their own affiliate programs in-house, but the majority now use agencies that serve as third-party managers, and many of the leading affiliate networks offer merchant support that automates verification, payment and monitoring. All the merchant has to do is occasionally provide banners or refreshed art to the third-party manager, although the best practice here is to actively recruit and groom your highest paid affiliates to continue to improve lead generation.

Figure 7-1 Sony's affiliate home page

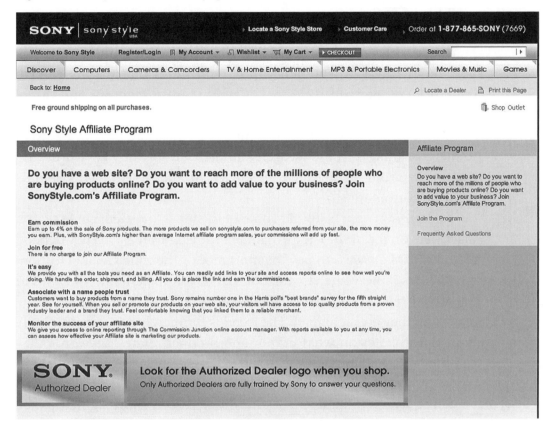

The best sites for affiliations have succeeded by having high-quality content or by superior knowledge of search marketing techniques. Around 2005 Google began making changes to its system to downgrade rank of sites that had duplicative content. This greatly affected affiliate sites, as much affiliate content inventory looked like duplicate content to Google's spiders. Certain sites were labeled "thin affiliates" and were either removed or downgraded. This resulted in smart affiliate marketers paying more attention to creating original quality content that provides a contextual environment, which improves conversions to the benefit of both sides.

AUTOMATED AFFILIATION: THE DARK SIDE OF SEARCH AFFILIATES

Many see a clear demarcation among affiliate sites that actively support the premise of lead generation, and those that passively serve links from a catch-all page that is only there to capture and direct clicks from a web search. While "content affiliates" attract audiences by offering a deep level of subject information before directing buyers to merchant pages, these "search affiliates" simply buy keywords and live on the arbitrage between the click cost and the affiliate sale payment on conversions.

In this group can be found some of the most knowledgeable search marketers on the Web. They live and breathe search 24/7. They depend on their SEM prowess to pay the mortgage or their kid's school tuition.

There is, however, a current controversy in the affiliate world as to the proper relationship between the search affiliates and the merchants for whom they are a channel. The trend is for merchants to increasingly limit the affiliates on what brand- and product-related keywords they can bid on or how high they can bid. This is to minimize potential bid competition between merchant and affiliate.

Some search affiliates maintain that this is a short-sighted policy and point out that, in the search affiliate model, it is the affiliates who are, in effect, financing the merchants' search marketing budget. Many merchants counter that the search affiliates "cannibalize" sales that should go directly to them. Advocates for the search affiliates maintain that they can be responsible for 10 to 30 percent of merchants' affiliate program sales, and that they provide the opportunity for merchants to gain traffic from multiple ads appearing on a search results page.

Some search affiliates may not even have a website, only a referring URL. While the search engines have rules about display URLs being the same as destination URLs, these are not always being followed. The number of rogue affiliates is probably low, but the issue is worrisome for merchants.

Affiliate marketing has largely gone unregulated and has inspired the industry to create standards of conduct. We have appended a widely observed conduct guideline that was originally agreed to by Commission Junction and Performics (now owned by Google). There have been efforts to create an industry association for affiliate marketing, but these have largely failed.

THE POWER OF THE NETWORK IS—WELL—THE POWER OF THE NETWORK

Affiliate marketing does more, however, than just provide merchant sites with an automated method of increasing sales leads. Many organizations, nonprofits, small startups, bloggers and industry services providers can use affiliation programs to gain a bit of revenue to monetize their websites, and there's even a nice halo effect when you are an affiliate to a larger organization, such as American Express, Sierra Club, or Amazon, to name but a few.

One of the most interesting conferences on all of Internet marketing is the Affiliate Summit (www.affiliatesummit.com). Much more "mom and pop" than other marketing gatherings, it is full of inspirational tales of folks who have created content-rich sites that profit from the affiliate model. Our favorite was the fellow who created a website showing off his knowledge of what makes the finest optical glass. He found, when he began recommending binoculars that used the finest glass that he could help sell over $70,000 worth of binoculars monthly. This has made him quite a player in the binocular universe.

Key Players in the Affiliate Marketplace

There are hundreds of affiliate networks. Let's take a look at the most important:

Commission Junction (www.cj.com). Commission Junction, owned by Value Click, is the largest affiliate network. Like the others, it provides solutions for merchants and publishers. Their two approaches are:

1. *CJ Marketplace (for publishers):* Commission Junction's network, the CJ Marketplace, provides publishers with opportunities to partner with leading advertisers. Commission Junction provides transparency by publishing the performance metrics of all advertisers, their respective ads as well as publishers within the CJ Marketplace. Strategic advice and featured weekly advertiser offers are available to CJ Marketplace publishers through CJU, a comprehensive online resource.

2. *CJ for Advertisers:* Advertisers partner with publishers to help promote their products and services to specific audiences, in exchange for commissions on leads or sales. CJ provides different tiers of service: CJ Access is a self-service solution that provides small to medium-sized advertisers access to CJ's network of publishers, plus educational resources and reporting tools. CJ Vantage is for medium and large advertisers, who get an assigned account manager to sustain publisher relationships, develop launch strategy and provide guidance.

ClickBank (www.clickbank.com). Founded in 1998, ClickBank is a primary source for digitally delivered products. From ebooks to software, ClickBank offers a vast array of digital goods. They have over 100,000 registered affiliates in their network, and over 10,000 product publishers. On a daily basis, ClickBank completes nearly 20,000 orders from more than 200 countries around the world.

Google Affiliate Network (formerly Performics) (www.google.com/ads/affiliatenetwork). Google has rebranded the Performics Affiliate Network, which it acquired when it purchased DoubleClick, so it is now the Google Affiliate Network. Merchant sites participating include those of Bank of America, Barnes & Noble, Citi, Target and Verizon. As before, there are programs for both publishers and advertisers.

Link Share (www.linkshare.com). LinkShare Corporation, founded in 1996, is the wholly owned U.S. division of Rakuten, Inc., a portal in Japan for shopping, online finance and travel, which claims to be the seventh largest Internet company in the world. LinkShare clients include J.C. Penney, 1–800-Flowers.com, American Express, Avon Products and Dell Computer Corporation.

Share A Sale (www.shareasale.com). Chicago-based Share A Sale offers a suite of services for merchants and publishers but has pricing that makes it more affordable than its rivals to get started as a merchant. They have over 2,000 merchants in their network.

THE DO-IT-YOURSELF AFFILIATE PROGRAM

There are also technologies available that allow merchants to manage their own affiliate programs. If you've got the technical expertise in-house or can outsource customization of off-the-shelf software, your options here include:

- *AssocTrac* (www.marketingtips.com/assoctrac/index.html): Assoc-TRAC is a web-based, two-tier affiliate software program for setting up a tracking system to promote your products and services. AssocTRAC integrates with most ordering systems and shopping carts, and was codeveloped by well-known Internet marketer Corey Rudl.

- *My Affiliate Program* (www.myaffiliateprogram.com): My Affiliate Program software (MyAP) is a scalable, customizable affiliate tracking and management solution that works with virtually every shopping cart and order processing system on the market. Setup is taken care of by the company within 24 hours.

FOR WEBSITE OWNERS AND PUBLISHERS: TECHNOLOGIES TO AUTOMATE AFFILIATE REVENUE

There are several technologies that make it easy to be an affiliate publisher that can pull inventory from such major product sources as ClickBank, Amazon and eBay:

- *Affiliates Alert* (www.affiliatesalert.com): This company offers a software program for searching the ClickBank product database. Features include sorting search results keywords, categories, subcategories, rankings and commission rates.

- *Build a Niche eBay Store (BANS)* (www.buildanichestore.com): BANS allows web publishers to automatically pull eBay listings into a website. Build A Niche Store currently supports eBay.com, eBay.co.uk, eBay.ca and eBay.com.au—meaning that you can build your own affiliate stores made up of products listed for sale in any one of these four marketplaces. Build a Niche Store revolves around eBay's hierarchical category structure. Once you have chosen the niche (category) you want to build your store around you simply enter that category number into the relevant part of your store setup area. For example, if you wanted to build a U.S. motorcycle store you would enter the category number 6024 and Build a Niche Store will automatically create your new affiliate website, which contains all of the motorcycles listed in that eBay category plus the associated subcategory navigation.

- *Associate O Matic* (www.associateomatic.com): Steve Rabuchin, Director of Developer Relations at Amazon, says, "Associate-O-Matic has leveraged the Amazon E-Commerce Service (Amazon ECS) to provide an easy-to-use store-building solution for Associates. This is innovative because they have built their offering on top of Amazon ECS, an Amazon Web Services developer API, in order to help Associates build powerful front-end websites quickly without having to be a developer themselves." In other words, if it's good enough for Amazon, it's probably good enough for you.

Where else can website owners look for affiliate programs right for them?

There are three options:

1. Google the names of merchants you would like to be part of. If you search for "Restoration Hardware Affiliate Program," you will find a link to the Restoration Hardware program. Most prominent merchants have affiliate programs and this method will find them, even if they are buried deep within the merchant site.

2. Search the usual suspects. Looking through the directories in Commission Junction, Share A Sale, DoubleClick and the other major affiliate networks will uncover the merchant programs in those categories.

3. Use the Affiliate Directories. You will find listed below the largest directories of merchant programs.

AffiliatesDirectory.com is one of the oldest Affiliate Programs Directories, dating back to 1998, and it lists more than 7,000 pay-per-sale, pay-per-click and pay-per-lead affiliate programs that offer two-tier and lifelong commissions. They also offer online educational resources and marketing tools for affiliates, including a free download of their ebook *Affiliate Master Course.*

AbestWeb.com is the world's largest affiliate marketing forum with more than 40,000 members and over 760,000 posts. They offer an Affiliate Academy, which covers the basics and updates in the industry, and a lively discourse on current topics.

Associate Programs (www.associateprograms.com/directory/) lists more than 10,000 programs. It is hosted by prominent Affiliate expert Allan Gardyne.

Affiliate Classroom (www.affiliateclassroom.com) offers online courses, a magazine and a blog (blog.affiliateclassroom.com). They have trained more than 12,000 students since January 2005.

BEST PRACTICES FOR AFFILIATE RELATIONSHIPS

Large merchant organizations typically designate an affiliates manager, who may captain a large department dedicated to improving inbound link traffic. Smaller companies should make this a responsibility of someone in the marketing department rather than in the community-building wing of public relations. This individual should be able to manage the relationship with the affiliate provider, in much the same way email firms and other web suppliers are handled, with a budget and a ROI target in mind.

As for mindset, you'll get the most out of your affiliates if you treat them as you would any other business partner: dig deep to discover your key affiliates, and give them special attention. If you can't take them out to dinner, at least identify your helpers and contact them personally once in a while, to thank them, give them advance notice of special promotions, or perhaps a product sample or a fruit basket at holiday time.

Updating banners, logo art or promotions through the seasons should be done routinely, and made a part of your marketing budget. And if 20 percent of your affiliates are generating 80 percent of your sales leads, keep building their business and drop the nonperformers.

Two of the largest affiliate networks, Commission Junction and Performics (now the Google Affiliate Network), promulgated Standards of Conduct for the Affiliate marketplace beginning in 2002. Although both parties have continued to update the "code" in light of their own marketplace realities, the basic principles have been embraced by many. We believe these are worthy guidelines that will give you an idea of what you can expect from a legitimate affiliation partner.

PUBLISHER CODE OF CONDUCT—
STILL A GOOD IDEA

When using the Service Provider's technology to obtain credit for publisher or affiliate referrals, the following actions, practices and conduct, whether active or passive, direct or indirect, are prohibited:

- *Interference with referrals.* No Web Publisher or software download Technology Provider may interfere with or seek to influence improperly the referral of a potential customer or visitor ("End-User") to the Web site of an online Advertiser. No Publisher or Technology Provider will automatically replace or alter any component of a Service Provider's technology that results in a reduction of any compensation earned by another Publisher. For example, a Publisher or Technology Provider may not use methods or technology to automatically replace a Service Provider's tracking identifier of another Publisher with its own Service Provider's tracking identifier or otherwise intercept or redirect an End-User from being referred through another Publisher's Link. Publisher may notify an End-User once that End-User has arrived at the Advertiser's Web site of an opportunity to utilize technology employed by that Publisher and obtain the End-User's consent via affirmative action upon each occurrence to proceed with the operation of such technology. Implementation of software application functionality requires that the notification be easily understood by the average End-User, that any settings for automatic notification must be explicitly opt-in, and that it is not objectionable to the Advertiser.

- *Non End-User Initiated Events.* Publishers may not use invisible methods to generate non End-User initiated impressions, clicks or transactions. All click ("Click") events must be initiated by an affirmative End-User action.
- *Altering another Publisher's site.* Publishers may not utilize Service Provider's technology in any manner that alters, changes, substitutes or modifies the content of another Publisher's Web pages.
- *Software installation and de-installation.* Publishers may not utilize Service Provider's technology with other Software, whereby the installation and deinstallation is not obvious, easy or complete. Licensing and terms of all software downloads and applications of any type must be clearly presented to and accepted by the End-User. Software that utilizes Service Provider's technology must be clearly marked in such a manner that the End-User can identify the Publisher's Software with an associated behavior that occurs on the End-User's computer, and receive visible notification of such behavior.

Definitions:

Advertiser—the company in an active relationship with a Service Provider for the purpose of displaying advertisements with Publishers to market their products and/or services

Publisher—the company in an active relationship with a Service Provider with which Advertiser's advertisements are displayed to End-Users

End-User—individuals (consumers) who respond to advertisements from Advertisers that are displayed by Publishers

Service Provider—a company that provides services and technologies to both Advertisers and Publishers

Technology Provider—the company that provides Software used to display Advertiser's advertisements to End-Users

Click—the initiation of an End-User referral action from a Publisher to an Advertiser's
   site, tracked through the Technology Provider's services

Publisher Link—a link to an Advertiser where an active affiliate relationship exists
   with one of the undersigned affiliate service providers and that:

Links to any of the following domains:

> bfast.com
>
> cc-dt.com
>
> qksrv.net
>
> commission-junction.com

(Note: these domains are subject to change based on technology change. Publishers
who are filtering these domains will be notified of changes.)

-or-

Contains a parameter named 'afsrc' set to any value.

e.g., http://www.mysite.com/redirect?offerid=12345&afsrc=1

This 'afsrc' parameter option is provided to address the case where affiliates modify
or mask the links provided to them from the affiliate service providers and it becomes
impossible to determine that they are affiliate links based on their appearance.

A Publisher Web Page is a page that contains a Publisher Link and is part of a website where an Advertiser and the Publisher have an active affiliate relationship.

First Published: December 10, 2002

Amended: February 10, 2003

Amended: August 12, 2004

[*Note from authors:* For further amendments and current status, a number of inde-
pendents keep this public domain material up to date, including Wikipedia and the following archive site: www.cumbrowski.com/CodeOfConduct.asp.]

PUBLIC RELATIONS 2.0

Moving Beyond the Traditional Media

PUBLIC RELATIONS is an arena where others ultimately determine your success or failure, no matter how you try. You could spend hours devising messaging strategies, work the phones and emails to build relationships with reporters and editors, or take advantage of relationships already built, to pitch the message. And then you hand control over to these reporters and editors who will make the determination as to whether or not the public, your customers, get an opportunity to hear or read your news. If they don't like it, you're toast. If there's a breaking news story, you're preempted toast.

This is how PR has traditionally been practiced, and sadly, how it still is done at many corporations and firms. PR's emphasis is almost solely on media relations and securing earned media coverage.

With Web 2.0, you have to change the way you think about PR. Consumers are choosing how, when and where they get news and information that is important to them. And, if your organization needs to reach out to a younger demographic, or a global marketplace, chances are good your target audience will ONLY see your message online. And, as we've found, the best way to communicate is directly to that target market using the web. Successful PR today means moving beyond "media relations" and into "direct to customer" relations. Do this successfully and you can ignore the mediators. Or, better yet, get them on board and chasing each other to cover your story, when online buzz levels reach a point where they can't ignore you for long.

Online, PR practitioners need to begin to think like word of mouth marketers. This can be frightening at first—but it is absolutely necessary that you, or your PR department or PR agency, have the skills to reach individuals on the web and to engage them, without the comforting cushion of mediators you have relied on in print, radio and TV. Adam Brown, director of digital communications for The Coca-Cola Company, emphasizes that corporate PR is about getting messages heard.

In their book, *The Influentials* (The Free Press, 2003), Ed Keller and Jon Berry posit that 1 in 10 people are "influentials." These superconsumers influence the other nine in how to vote, what to buy, etc. The most stunning statistic from DoubleClick's landmark Touchpoint IV Focus Report (www.doubleclick.com/insight/pdfs/dc_influencers_0612.pdf) was that influentials spend more time on the Internet than they do with television, radio, magazines and newspapers combined. As a PR professional, you can't ignore this consumer segment.

Why have influential consumers increasingly turned away from traditional media?

- *Convenience*. Consumers can get news and information on any screen at any time they want it, on multiple platforms, such as an iPod, mobile phone or text pager.

- *Relevance*. Consumers can choose the news that is most interesting to them during any time of day; they no longer have to wait for a morning newspaper or an 11:00 newscast. A B-to-B customer can sign up for email alerts for a particular industry, and surf the web to shop on a lunch hour.

- *Depth.* Consumers can drill down to the level of detail they want on a particular topic. Using search, it's possible to amass quantities of information; links and tags on news stories allow skimming related stories with a single click.

Another element is the homogenization of traditional media. In her doctoral thesis, "The Effects of Ownership: A Case Study of Cross Owned and Non Cross Owned Media Outlets in a Single Local Market," Dr. Susan Lewis, assistant professor of journalism and mass communication at Abilene Christian University, found that newspapers, television and radio stations and their associated websites *all carried basically the same news*. While her research was focused on determining if single corporate ownership of newspaper, television and radio outlets in a local market influenced or homogenized the news delivered to consumers by those local media in the same "family," she found that there was not a significant difference in what the other, independently owned media in the same market covered. It's no wonder then that consumers are exploring other, more global avenues for news and information.

In a Google search of key words representing the top five most searched news stories of 2007, Wikipedia ranked higher than the *New York Times* website four out of five times. [*Source:* http://www.cadenhead.org/workbench/news/3302/long-bet-winner-weblogs-vs-new-york]

As consumers are tuning out traditional media, they're tuning in to the new outlets available on the Internet like blogs, RSS feeds, podcasts, social networks and web video.

Additionally, compared to the number of traditional outlets available for PR efforts, the Internet provides exponentially more outlets for news and information. The way to reach consumers is to engage influentials in conversation, to focus on facilitating their abilities to become evangelists for your brand.

In the remainder of this chapter, we'll cover specific strategies to create conversation with citizen journalists as well as with online forms of traditional media.

COZYING UP TO BLOGGERS

User-generated content has always been the biggest traffic driver on the web. From the early web to today, that hasn't changed. AOL was huge in the mid-1990s, and the bulk of their traffic came from users congregating in chat channels and socializing. There were active participants and there were lurkers, who like cybervoyeurs would just read the repartee between chatters and never participate. Sites like GeoCities and Xing provided early tools to enable consumers to start building their own pages and write about anything that interested them, thus breaking the channel structure of predetermined areas of interest.

Web logs, now called "blogs," evolved out of the social chat applications that were so popular on the early web at AOL and similar sites, and out of the early social networks that enabled consumers to create their own pages; facilitators such as TypePad (www.typepad.com) simplified the technology even more.

Blogs provide a window to the world of individuals. For some, like artists or inner-city youth who tag buildings and vehicles with graffiti to make their mark and get noticed, a personal blog represents an escape from anonymity. For others, a blog is their private journal, open to the world. By posting their innermost thoughts and concerns, they are perhaps hoping that others with similar thoughts and struggles will connect with them.

Naturally, bloggers with perspicacity and a clear voice have emerged and obtained a following. Some of these have become a new breed of citizen journalist who wields as much power as any major newspaper columnist.

Keeping the old media relations hat on for a moment, connecting with key bloggers is really not that different from connecting with other journalists. It is a four-step process:

1. *First, do the research to find the bloggers that serve your audience.* Technorati.com is one place to start, although a majority of posts are likely to be irrelevant. Google's Blog Search (www.blogsearch .google.com) is perhaps more up to date. On their system you can, and should, set up a Google Alert (www.google.com/alerts) with your company's URL and company name, to find out who is talking about you in the blog space. Remember, you don't necessarily need to find bloggers with a large audience—you need to find bloggers with the *right* audience.

2. *Next, read their posts, learn their likes and dislikes.* This is known as "lurking" and is highly recommended. You must resist the temptation to reply immediately to any perceived slur about your company— it proves much more useful to let a comment string play out, and continue to watch the postings and their responses over a period of time to discover weaknesses, champions, preferences and pinpoint those bloggers and those commentators who are sympathetic to your message and can serve as influentials.

3. *When you feel you are ready, get engaged in the blog.* Respond to items written on the blog by offering feedback or comments in postings on the blog. Best practice suggests that you not pitch your product or service, but instead, offer advice or a link to a source that relates to the issue discussed. For example, if you sell ski equipment and a ski blog discussion on waxed versus nonwaxed skis starts up, the best link to proffer might be to a part of your website that compares performance of the two. Check out these real-world examples from a small enterprise

vendor (www.skiwax.ca/tp/waxless.php) and from a large one (www.xc-skiworld.com/equip/equip_classic.htm#wax_or_waxless).

You get the idea: communicating in blogs is, yes, about ideas and information sharing—this is how the Internet learns to beat a path to your door.

4. *Finally, create real relationships with the blogger.* Provide materials or other sources that you may have. PR is all about relationships and dialogue. Blogging, and the mechanisms inherent in the technology for response, feedback and instant posting, can make developing relationships and creating dialogue much easier with a blogger than with a traditional journalist.

Use bloggers sparingly but feed their appetite for the juicy news bit. Bloggers in your industry are perfect for "leaking" new product news in advance of an official press release date. Bloggers are highly competitive, and will race to be the first to post a good story. Provide artwork such as product shots and you'll improve your chances for a posting.

There are risks with relying on bloggers—they have no editorial review board, and some enjoy leaning toward the anarchistic side—but their impact with key communities cannot be denied. Do the risk analysis yourself, but if you successfully harness the power of the bloggers important to your audience, you'll win.

EXAMPLE: NETFLIX FLOGS, THEN EMBRACES THE BLOG

Netflix is a great company many of us know and love. It has an extensive audience of loyal users. One such user, Mike Kaltschnee, was so committed that he created a blog about Netflix (www.hackingnetflix.com). He was considering starting a blogging initiative at his day job because, as he put it, "press releases weren't working, we needed to communicate directly with our consumers."

The Netflix blog was his research or experiment to learn about blogging. His blog became so popular that readers began to come to him with questions for the company. Realizing he could help the company with consumer insight, Mike emailed the PR department at Netflix asking for their help with an "Ask Netflix" story, so that they could address their customers' questions. In response, he received a form letter thanking him for his inquiry, but telling him that Netflix declined to participate. Disappointed, he posted his original inquiry, and their response on his blog. This created a firestorm of posts to his blog and angry emails to Netflix. To their credit, Netflix quickly realized the reach and influence of this blogger and promoted him to A-list media status, and opened connections for him with key people within the company. This all happened within one week of his posting the form letter.

Mike continues to enjoy insider access to Netflix, reviewing new interfaces and online products. "I'm just amazed that a company as huge as Netflix will spend time with a guy who works out of his basement," relates Mike. He astutely adds, "Blogging isn't necessarily about how many readers you have, or how much attention your blog gets, it's a matter of influence. Bloggers form communities around them and thus command huge influence with their readers. Smart companies realize this and respect the influence some bloggers can wield." With 250,000 readers per month, he definitely wields some influence.

Don't interpret the previous discourse as simply transferring the same media relations rules to a different medium. The power of the Internet, as stated earlier, is the ability to go around mediators and engage more directly with consumers. You can create your own blog within minutes and begin making direct, one-to-one connections with your customers.

SHOULD YOU HAVE YOUR OWN BLOG?

There are several advantages to creating and maintaining your own blog:

- *Provide unfiltered information.* Your information and expertise are directly available to your audience. There are no mediators interpreting, or misinterpreting, your information. The salient points get through.

- *Enjoy direct access to your consumers' focus.* By allowing readers to post feedback, or comments to your blog entries, you will invariably gain valuable insight into the likes and dislikes of your consumers. You will learn how they relate to your product, and what modifications they would most like to see.

- *Become a prime resource.* Your objective is to be top of mind among your consumers when their need for your particular product or service arises. A blog helps you to position yourself and your company as experts in the field.

- *Increase your ranking in the world of search engines.* One metric search engines measure when determining the relevance of a particular site is the number of inbound links to that site. The more inbound links, the higher the site ranks on the search engine. Blogs create links to your site by others linking to and referencing your blog, and by you creating links to your site within your blog.

Technorati, the top blog search engine, estimates that 120,000 blogs are created every day, so it obviously isn't that complicated to get a blog up and going. There are simple community sites like blogger.com or xanga.com where you sign up and start blogging. On an enterprise level, there are companies like Six Apart, Inc. (www.sixapart.com), which provide blogging platforms from the shared-consumer level with Vox (www.vox.com), all the way up to the large enterprise, fully integrated level with Movable Type (www.movabletype.com). Most web hosting providers have some kind of blogging and community application built-in, or available for a small additional fee. There are also a number of freeware blogging applications your IT department could down-

load from the web and customize. As you can see, there are really no
technology or financial barriers to your having a blog up and running
quickly.

When contemplating a blogging solution, there are several important factors to consider for maximum PR effectiveness:

- *Indexing.* One of the key advantages of maintaining a blog is its
  ability to elevate your website and your message in the top search
  engines. Make sure that your blog application inserts the proper
  tags to make your blog visible and indexable by Google, Yahoo!,
  Ask.com and MSN. "Claim" your blog on Technorati.com, to get it
  listed there as well.

- *Multimedia.* You will need the ability to add photographs, audio
  and video podcasts and PowerPoint presentations, at the very
  least. This interactivity will more readily serve your needs, and
  will make the blog more appealing.

- *Syndication.* Your blog needs to be enabled for RSS (more on RSS
  in the next section of this chapter) feeds so that news aggregators
  and consumers can more easily find you and tap into your
  information.

One difficulty many company bloggers have is getting out of the
press release box. The Internet is a "tell me, don't sell me" medium. Remember, we can't all be the Apple iPhone. You may find that a blog ad-
dressing concerns common in your consumer segment at large is more
effective than a blog that talks about your products or services. Think
about how you can become indispensable to your community. As soon
as a blog entry becomes too commercial, a consumer's B-S-ometer
spikes into the red zone, their filters engage and your credibility is out
the window. The objective is to become a trusted, reliable source, the
center of the universe. To do this, you must provide the most relevant

information, the most comprehensive information and the least commercial information.

The other major pitfall for organizational or corporate blogs is that someone must be available to create fresh postings to keep the conversation going. Outsourcing to freelancers (found through job networking sites such as mediabistro.com or elance.com) is a common solution. Payment is either by retainer or by the post; compensation may also take into account traffic levels as pay-per-performance carrot and stick. If you're lucky, someone on staff will have the knack and the skill and be suitable as a spokesperson for your blog.

McDonald's took this a step further into the realm of community engagement, by enrolling six women in the Mom's Quality Correspondent program. The company sent out an email blast soliciting participants and culled through the 4,000 applicants to come up with six demographically diverse moms, who became bloggers for the site (www.mcdonaldsmom.com). As one goal was to change perceptions of the company's food quality and address urban myths, the correspondents were given full access to McDonald's preparation, supply chain and management in their areas. Their reviews and impressions were then regularly posted on the McDonald's blog. More than 14,000 consumers enrolled to read the blog, and countless others followed the six moms as other blogs across the web began carrying the McDonald's posts. This program is now in its second year.

RSS FEEDS AND THEIR USE IN PUBLIC RELATIONS

As early as 1995, enterprising entrepreneurs spoke of a future where all news would be customized; where consumers could empower intelligent agents to comb the web and retrieve only the news items that were relevant to them. As in most cases, the early pioneers were the ones who ended up with arrows in their backs. However, their prophecies have become reality with today's RSS.

Tips to Keep Your Own Blog in the Spotlight

Blog often. At least three times a week—and five times a week is even better. Several times a day is best of all. Your blog posts don't have to be long, and they don't have to be information-packed. In fact, they don't have to be about you (see next item about borrowing content). You must give audiences a reason to check in frequently, and nothing turns a potential reader off more than the phrase: "Last Update Nov. 3, 2007."

Borrow good content. If you don't have enough to fill out a week's worth of entries, look around the web and link out to sites or other bloggers in your topic area. Linking also helps other bloggers "see" you—and they are more likely to link back to your blog if you've posted something flattering about their ideas or timely posts.

Read other blogs in your topic area and post comments. When you post a comment, type in your blog or website's URL (within the comment block) so it will show up as a link. This is one area where you don't have to be afraid to disagree with the original blogger (politely of course). Often, readers are lurking but will visit your blog if your comments align with their interests.

Attending blogging conventions is also helpful to build up a network for your blog. South by Southwest (SXSW) is the largest nationally, and there are regional and topic conferences as well (www.sxsw.com/interactive).

RSS stands for "Really Simple Syndication" and it is basically a group of web applications that will automatically collect and republish frequently updated website content—such as blog postings, news headlines, or news stories. RSS enables you to make your website reach a broader audience, by making your site indexable by search engines and RSS aggregators. It makes it easier for your web videos, presentations, audios, blogs, websites and press releases to be noticed, accessed, picked up, formatted and redistributed across the web.

Figure 8-1 Mobilecrunch, a blog site for a business

As a PR professional, RSS provides you with several key applications: dissemination, aggregation and research.

RSS Can Spread Your Message

In the world where you bypass mediators to reach your consumer, RSS is a valuable weapon in your arsenal. When releasing news on your website, you simply need to incorporate the proper tags for your news to be readable or visible to **RSS** readers.

Press release distribution services like **PR Newswire** are already adding the proper coding, enabling releases sent through their service to be propagated across the web very quickly. An interesting consequence of this is that as more consumers are reading press releases, their stigma of being biased corporate news is being diluted. A research study of 7,000 knowledge workers conducted from 2004 to 2006 by Outsell, Inc. (www.outsellinc.com), a syndicated research and advisory firm for companies in the information industry, has found that press releases are the most preferred source of company information.

And, more than just text can be syndicated. iTunes for example provides the option of adding **RSS** to your video and audio podcasts. YouTube allows you to subscribe to videos and series so that you get notified when the next installment is posted. Social networks update groups of friends when new content is added to a social page.

Taking the "kingmaker" power of blogs one step further, **RSS** enables your site to be a news or content aggregator. This enhances your site and provides one more compelling reason for customers to visit your web pages. By doing the research and committing the resources, you can pull together news and information about your industry and other topics relevant to your consumer base. This will drive traffic to your site and further establish your expertise in your particular market segment. Don't be afraid to skew toward niche marketing with your news site or page. If you strive to appeal to all, you usually end up appealing to none. Conversely, if you shrewdly aggregate only the most relevant content on your site, your traffic may be less but you improve your chances of reaching the most highly targeted and motivated audience for your marketing message.

There are a number of **RSS** applications you can use to help you pull news together and post it on your site. Newsgator (www.newsgator.com), is perhaps the largest **RSS** products company, and thus offers the most services for a turnkey solution. There are, however, a number of **RSS** readers that are very robust, and free. With a little research, you may find a no-cost solution that meets all of your needs with a little extra work on your end. Do a Google search on "RSS readers" or "RSS aggregators" to begin your quest.

RSS as a Feedback Tool

Finally, RSS is an incredibly valuable market research and intelligence-gathering tool. At Hardin-Simmons University (HSU), David Coffield, director of public relations, and Leland Harden, vice president of institutional advancement (and coauthor of this book), found that with effective monitoring of RSS feeds, searching for references to the university rendered their clipping service virtually obsolete. The clipping service occasionally delivered references from small, community newspapers missed by RSS monitoring, but based on timeliness and relevance, it became apparent that the monthly fee being spent on the clipping service was better utilized elsewhere.

The main search engines and Internet providers all have RSS readers and channels. Simply go to their respective home pages and either click on the RSS link, or search "RSS reader." You will then need to select the channels or content categories you feel are most appropriate, and experiment with the key word search terms to find the ones that deliver the best results. The key word terms you've used for search marketing might be a good place to begin. Start narrow and then expand. If your search terms are too broad, you'll likely discover that it's like trying to get a drink from a fire hydrant: you'll quench your thirst, but you may drown in the process.

RSS readers are also built into Internet browsers. You may find that simply by tweaking your browser, you'll have access to everything you'll need.

There are commercial RSS readers that charge a fee, like Newsgator referenced above, but as David Coffield puts it, "the commercial readers didn't provide enough upside, either in content delivered or ease of use, to warrant paying for them." The only caveat may be that certain readers may have access to proprietary content channels such as expensive research reports and technical data, which could make paying a fee a sound investment.

As you research the readers you want to use, think about convenience and content. Some will deliver results right into your email inbox, others will provide a customized page for you to access whenever you want to. In the end, you'll likely want to end up with three or four different sources you check on a regular basis. You'll find that they have areas where they overlap and provide common results, as well as certain sources that appear in only one or another. You should set up a Google Alert (www.google.com/alerts) to specifically catch news items about you or your company, and perhaps with three or four more. With a battery of RSS readers working for you, you'll catch about 98 percent or more of the news on the web you're looking for

The advantages of using RSS for nonprofits are many. HSU has found stories about long-lost alumni and discovered ways to reconnect with them, as well as stories about students or alumni that are being covered elsewhere. The latter has enabled the university to leverage that news for coverage in additional markets and channels. Finally, HSU has been able to gain a much better understanding of its footprint on the Internet, and where it stands in the competitive landscape. If your CEO has ever been blindsided by a story on the Internet, RSS is one way for you and your company to minimize surprises.

PODCASTS

When Apple Computer reinvented the music industry with the introduction of the iPod and the iTunes music store, it is likely that Steve Jobs and the other geniuses at Apple knew the power of their platform, but no one else in the business world could have predicted the impact they would have. With well over 100 million iPods in the marketplace and the iTunes music store eclipsing CD sales, to say Apple has achieved critical mass would be an understatement. iPodders are a vast, diverse and engaged community you can effectively tap for your communications strategy.

The term podcast is the derivation of combining POD, the acronym for portable-on-demand, with broadcast. A podcast is a prerecorded audio or video program that is most commonly posted on iTunes, but can also be posted on your website, your social media site or other podcast aggregation sites. These programs take a number of forms: personal video blogs (vlogs), amateur radio shows, talk shows, PowerPoint presentations with voice-over, news stories, video news releases, amateur television shows, short films and full-length motion pictures. "Live" podcasts are common today; the imagination is truly the only limit.

As a corporate communicator, you can easily produce and release audio or video podcasts. The best way to do this is, we're sorry to break the news to you PC dedicatees, is with a Mac. Garageband is an audio creation and editing application that comes preinstalled on every Mac and seamlessly integrates with iTunes. Tutorials are available, but basically you can import music, record a voice-over, drop in slides if you like and then export it to iTunes. RSS feed key word information will be requested and after a few clicks you're in business.

There are also other podcasting communities across the web that provide all of the tools for creating and uploading a podcast and its associated RSS information. MyPodcast.com and podomatic.com are two such sites. There are any number from which to choose. Just search "create a podcast" and you'll find a few days' worth of sites to comb through with tutorials, tips and tools to test. Make sure that whatever you do, you upload your podcast to iTunes. Other sites may host tons of podcast material, but Apple has the largest audience by far. It's not necessary to go exclusively with iTunes, far from it, but whatever you do, don't exclude it.

For video podcasts, research released by the Pew Internet and American Life Project in July 2007 indicates that consumers prefer professionally produced video over amateur video. The report found that, overall, online video viewers preferred content created by professionals and not amateurs. Over 60 percent of the 2,200 adults involved in the study expressed a preference for videos produced by professionals. Nineteen percent preferred to watch videos made by amateurs. "However," says the report, "the segments that do express a preference for amateur content or say they like both genres equally is sizable, and those who are among the most coveted viewers by advertisers (men ages 18–29) are the most likely to express a preference for amateur video." So if you want your video to have legs, spend the necessary dollars to do it well.

For the do-it-yourselfers, there are a number of programs to create video podcasts, ranging in complexity and sophistication. Macs come preinstalled with iMovie, and Final Cut Pro is a slick professional tool for Mac users. Adobe and Avid make products for both the PC and the Mac platforms.

Podcasts can range from being an audio or video blog, all the way to being a human interest radio-type show with special guests. One of the best examples of a corporate podcast program can be found on the Whirlpool site at Whirlpool.com. The podcasts were the brainchild of Audrey Reed-Granger, director of public relations at Whirlpool. Moving beyond product podcasts, which are on the site, Whirlpool has created a strong series of human interest podcasts relevant to their target audience—moms—and has posted them on their site. The series is called "American Family" and has developed a deep library of relevant content and, based on the number of downloads—some in the hundreds of thousands, a deep and loyal audience.

When considering a podcast program, address the following:

- *Be relevant.* In this word of mouth marketing world, you need to constantly be asking yourself, "Is this worth talking about?" And then "Is this worth talking about right now?" If it's not, rethink your topics. Your objective is to engage your consumer in conversation. This may mean that, like the American Family podcasts, your programming isn't always about your products.

- *Think about your consumer's lifestyle.* This can affect the type of content you deliver, as well as the vehicle you use to deliver it. A video podcast requires active engagement, where an audio podcast can be played in the background while other tasks are being completed.

- *Archive your podcasts,* or at least the ones you're proudest of, on your site.

PROMOTIONAL VIDEO

Television, radio and newspaper websites are all carrying video, and asking consumers to contribute video. Video is no longer the realm of television stations. Video sites can be found all across the web: YouTube, every major search engine, television, radio, newspaper websites, MySpace pages, Facebook pages and many others. One simple search on the video search engine, Blinkx.com, will show you the plethora of content and sources. Companies and commercial enterprises are actively jumping into the online video fray, as most of them have already had experience in providing "video press releases," otherwise known as a VNR or "B-Roll," to support a new product or venture.

Edward Lamoureaux, senior vice president of West Glen Communications, a corporate video production and distribution company in New York City, has found that media companies, as well as social media sites and sites that serve niche communities, are eager to utilize video relevant to their audience on their sites. The most common complaint is professionalism—content aggregators prefer professionally produced video over amateur video.

Rachel Meranus, vice president of public relations at MultiVu, PR Newswire's broadcast arm, says "web video is taking precedence over television" among their clients. Since the Federal Communications Commission ruled on April 13, 2005, that television stations must fully disclose their use of corporate-sponsored video, most television news departments have refused to use any video news releases or VNRs, for fear of fines. With the proliferation of video on the web, the VNR technique of producing complete news packages, or complete stories, is being applied online.

"We're finding that stories can be more interesting online, and we can target our audience much more tightly," says Meranus. "We encourage clients to make their stories tighter, more fast-paced, and a little quirkier." Since attention spans can be more limited online, videos must capture the attention of the viewer more quickly.

Viewers are voting with their mouse-clicks. Professionally produced videos are far outpacing amateur videos in terms of downloads. Marc Newman, divisional vice president for MultiVu, adds, "Content matters. The more interesting the story, the more the downloads." This offers an extraordinary opportunity for marketers to learn from their audience. You can monitor the number of times a video is viewed and learn what messages or products resonate with consumers.

BLENDED MEDIA: PUT SOME PAY INTO YOUR PR

Edward Lamoureaux, a veteran of the corporate public relations video industry, as well as the Internet industry, has devised tactics that wed PR and the web very effectively. He calls this "blended media."

Blended media is defined as the use of *all* available marketing and media channels (earned media, paid media, social media and direct-to-consumer PR tactics) to drive awareness for a message and to reach intended audiences utilizing PR and word of mouth context and tactics.

He utilizes audience development tactics for his clients in his public relations video placement practice. "Audience development" is a term coined by the authors of this book in 1994 to represent the cohesive online marketing tools and methodologies they developed to build some of the most powerful brands on the Internet. In a nutshell, audience development is defined as identifying your most relevant audiences, pinpointing where those audiences are spending their time (on television, the radio and the Internet) and then driving those audiences to your messages with integrated multimedia campaigns.

Figure 8-2 A public relations banner

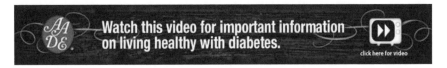

Figure 8-3 A nonprofit's branding banner

Perhaps the most unique innovation to the tactics discussed previously in this chapter are Lamoureaux's utilization of PR messaging in online advertising banners to drive click-through. Here are some examples of advertising banners that use PR messaging, instead of advertising messaging.

The industry standard for click-through rates on advertising banners still hover around 0.25 percent. That means that for every 100 times an advertising banner is served up on a web page, it actually results in a click one-quarter of one percent of the time. According to Lamoureaux, banners with PR messaging are seeing click-through rates five to six times the industry average.

Most PR professionals do not see paid media placement as part of their purview, but there's no denying its effectiveness.

So, according to Lamoureaux (and we heartily concur), for best re-sults you should utilize all of the available outlets you can muster to gain placement of your corporate video, free placements on video sites and within key communities, and paid placements on commercial sites, then drive traffic to your video through audience development tactics by engaging your communities and key placement of paid media across relevant websites.

PUTTING IT ALL TOGETHER: THE MULTIMEDIA NEWS RELEASE

Now that you're a word-of-web-direct-to-consumer-engagement spe-cialist, you have to rethink how you do a press release. You know that what you really need is the new improved version—the multimedia news release.

According to PR Newswire's site, "a Multimedia News Release (or 'MNR') is an interactive news release with video, audio, still photos, and text. . . . In essence, the MNR is a 'one-stop shop' for journalists, con-sumers, clients, investors, and anyone else who wants to get as much information as they can about a news story."

A great example of a multimedia news release is actually on PR Newswire's website (www.prnewswire.com/mnr).

Here are the elements of a multimedia news release:

- *Press release.* The traditional press release isn't going away. It just has extra features attached to it with the MNR. Make sure your press release has contact information, links to email addresses and websites. If your news is timely, make sure at least one of those email addresses is for a team member who will be able to respond 24/7, because online media does not take weekends off or go home at 5 p.m. Eastern. Make sure that your release is RSS-enabled and search engine–optimized either by your press release distribution service or by following the steps outlined below to garner the best proliferation across the web.

- *Online video.* As said previously, video is no longer exclusive to television news stations or their respective websites. Video is carried on newspaper, radio and magazine sites, as well as countless other corporate community sites and social network pages. In order to enable television stations to use your video on air, you will need to make two versions available from your MNR, one that is broadcast quality (mpeg 2) and one that is Internet ready (Flash). Make sure that a link to embed your video on other sites is posted with your video, as well as the option to forward it to others.

- *Mobile content.* Repurpose your video so that it is compatible with distribution to mobile phones. PR Newswire uses U-Turn Mobile Media Group (www.u-turnmediagroup.com).

- *Audio release.* Some of your customers may want an audio podcast that they can post on their sites or share with their friends. As with video, provide a link to embed the audio release or forward it to others.

- *Photos.* Provide high-resolution photos (600 dpi) for traditional publications to download and use, and faster-loading web resolutions (72 dpi) for bloggers and your customers to use, if they so wish.

- *Related Links.* If there are blog postings about your product, a social media page or other areas across the web that tie into the topic of your release, provide links to them.

- *Social media.* Provide links to tie your MNR into the most popular social media sites. This will enable your community to essentially "vote" on your release and aid in its distribution across the web.

How to Optimize a Press Release for Search

Want more exposure for your published web press release? Take a page from the *Wall Street Journal* and the *New York Times*, and optimize your release with keywords that will bring it up more often in searches of your topic on search engines. At the *Journal*, headline writers are taught to use phrasings that crop up in searches of key topics. At About.com, an information site run by the *New York Times* and written by free-lancers, new writers are given a style sheet that shows them how to invest headlines and first paragraphs with grouped keywords, so they pop up in a specific search: "how to mow a lawn," "mow a lawn" and "mow lawn," etc.

Optimizing a release for search makes it more accessible to the target audience that does not know you by name. Once they've found you, make it easy for both the press and your customer community to replicate and pass around the assets, with a widget, for example, or a useful email link. Make your release extensible by providing as many tools as possible to your community to empower them to spread the word for you.

CASE STUDY: **Toyota's Branding in the Blog Space Aims for Conversations, Not Conversions**

Bruce Ertmann, director of consumer-generated media at Toyota Motor Sales (TMS) USA, says the genesis of his position within the company was more of a revolution than an evolution. A 20-year veteran of the company, Bruce was asked to spearhead a consumer-generated media (CGM) research project for the corporate communications group. The resulting white paper he produced had several recommendations, one of which was the creation of the role he now holds.

Toyota's consumer-generated media initiative began in earnest in 2006 with Bruce actively engaging consumers on the web. He started with enthusiast sites and forums for Toyota like PriusChat.com (www.priuschat.com) and ToyotaNation.com (www.toyotanation.com), among others. This wasn't a stealth operation or some covert guerilla marketing initiative, both of which could lead to disastrous ends if discovered, so Bruce joined the online groups as TMSUSA. He was the online voice of the company.

"Initially, there was skepticism among some of the consumer groups, but as they learned that my role was to responsibly participate, to provide insight into issues and to be transparent, truthful and authentic, their trust increased significantly, and the initiative became a very positive force for the company," said Bruce. "Toyota is a good brand, so building trust has been much easier."

A corporate blogging initiative is a hybrid animal, it crosses over between reputation management and corporate communications. Therefore, it must be voiced from a consumer perspective and avoid corporate speak. It must be more conversational. The primary objective is not to do damage control, but to be aware of what is being said about the company, its products, and its community initiatives—to engage customers in conversation.

Beyond the Toyota enthusiast sites, Bruce went to the powerhouse car research site Edmunds.com (www.edmunds.com) and established a forum. The folks at Edmunds were thrilled with this proactive initiative, as it was the first major car company to do so.

By being plugged in, Bruce found he was able to discover issues with vehicles and dealer communications and address them directly. "We wouldn't have known if we weren't engaged." Further, "I was able to document how being upfront and transparent with the consumer, confronting any problems, I was able to turn what could have been significantly negative events among customers into catalysts for creating goodwill and enhance the positive image of Toyota," related Bruce.

As the word got out, other sites began to link to his posts, so his message spread virally.

It soon became apparent that simply participating in others' blogs might not be enough. A misleading review of a Toyota vehicle's safety rating needed to be confronted directly, and the third-party enthusiast blogs did not provide a relevant platform. So, after overcoming initial resistance from internal media relations traditionalists—assuring them that a Toyota blog was not meant to replace traditional media relations, it would serve only to enhance them—Toyota launched the Toyota Open Road Blog (www.toyotaopenroadblog.com) in June 2007.

The company intentionally kept their blog separate from the corporate site and created a separate identity for it. "We didn't want it to be viewed as a corporate spin machine. We felt having a little space between the corporate site and the blog made the blog more credible."

The TMS blog is open. It allows consumers to post comments, provide feedback and ask questions. Comments are screened, mostly to keep bad language and inappropriate posts out, but Toyota lets most go through. This creates an atmosphere of active engagement and conversation with customers and other key industry and government contacts.

The Toyota blogging initiative has been very successful. Customers have been pleased, if not surprised, to find a company that listens to their concerns, addresses issues in a transparent, forthright manner and breaks the mold of a faceless corporate behemoth. The company has found that customers will tell them what they want, and by simply listening, they can better address their needs and solidify relationships.

Lessons from the Road of Experience

1. *Do your homework.* Bruce studied the blogs of tech companies to learn more about how they were relating to their customers. You may choose to research the Toyota blog and other corporate

blogs as well to better refine the scope and mission of your blog initiative.

2. *Be willing to be transparent.* The purpose of a corporate blogging initiative is not solely to defend the company, but to clarify untruths and rumors circulating on the web. Don't ever try to be a stealth operation, or assume bogus consumer identities. A blog enables you to address problems head on, and gain considerable trust and goodwill from your consumers. "If you've got a problem, get out there and talk about it!"

3. *Be willing to be open.* Many companies make blogs a glorified bulletin board by not allowing comments to be posted. This is like a one-way conversation, you may feel good about everything you said, but you didn't learn anything in the process. While it can be uncomfortable at times, don't be afraid to publish commentary. You don't have to publish negative flame posts, but outright censorship goes against the tenets of blogs. You'll discover that your community can be self-policing. If a topic goes too far afield, community participants will bring it back on course with healthy debate. You'll find your community selling themselves.

4. *Be willing to take risks.* Like in any relationship, between individuals and between companies and their consumers, there are risks associated with being so public, so transparent. Taking time to educate your legal department in advance, enrolling them in the process, can lead to better cooperation down the line. It's probably not necessary to run every post by legal before you hit the publish button, but keep your controversy meter finely tuned and show legal those posts that have even a wisp of controversy by them. This will elicit a better relationship with your legal group, and keep you from having to backtrack in public. The legal group knows what litigation is pending and can keep you from putting your foot in the middle of it.

C H A P T E R   9

PAID MEDIA

Advertising Works Harder on the Web

Rudy Giuliani spent $60 million on his presidential campaign and won only one delegate.

—NEWSWEEK (FEBRUARY 15, 2007)

WHAT'S THE MOST EFFECTIVE MEDIUM for paid advertisements? Depends on who you talk to. A 2007 survey of 2,000 online marketers found that 80 percent of them felt that email marketing was the most effective use of their media dollars, compared to 37 percent who felt that banner advertisements were equally or more effective. Less than 2 percent gave credit to mobile advertising platforms. The study was undertaken by, no surprise, Datatran, an agency that services the email marketing industry.

Meanwhile, a survey of 270 broadcast advertising executives discovered that, while 90 percent agreed with a statement that Internet distribution would account for 40 percent of all video content by 2012, two-thirds of the execs surveyed agreed that TV would still host 60 percent of all video consumption by consumers for at least the next five years. That study was underwritten by Teletrax, a global broadcast ratings and monitoring agency that is partly owned by Philips Electronics, which happens to make television monitors.

Another perspective on where advertising dollars are going comes from eMarketer, which projects growth in ad spending, as shown in Figure 9-1.

But, if you were only interested in following the crowd, you wouldn't be reading this book.

Figure 9-1 Where online marketers put their ad dollars

US Online Advertising Spending, by Format, 2008-2013 (millions)

	2008	2009	2010	2011	2012	2013
Search	$10,396	$11,885	$13,869	$16,605	$20,375	$23,777
Display ads	$5,210	$5,919	$6,857	$8,144	$9,425	$10,012
Classifieds	$3,710	$4,218	$4,925	$5,913	$7,200	$8,319
Video	$505	$750	$1,150	$1,900	$3,400	$5,800
Lead generation	$1,868	$2,109	$2,429	$2,936	$3,500	$4,071
Rich media	$1,967	$2,195	$2,580	$2,957	$3,550	$4,012
Sponsorships	$772	$912	$1,106	$1,377	$1,800	$2,183
E-mail	$473	$513	$586	$668	$750	$826
Total	**$24,900**	**$28,500**	**$33,500**	**$40,500**	**$50,000**	**$59,000**

Note: eMarketer benchmarks its US online advertising spending projections against the Interactive Advertising Bureau (IAB)/PricewaterhouseCoopers (PwC) data, for which the last full year measured was 2007
Source: eMarketer, August 2008

097139 www.eMarketer.com

THE EVOLUTION OF WEB ADVERTISING

Paid online media had its first revolution when advertisers realized that actual numbers could be returned and reviewed for performance. It had the second when advertisers realized that banner click-through rates could not predict conversions. And today, it is clear that click-through rates by themselves are a meaningless statistic, and merely a guidepost to where your money should be going online.

Still, you create the ad. An agency (or in-house equivalent) places the ad. The third-party ad servers deliver and track the ad. Comscore, Quantcast and other companies count the size of the audiences of the media properties. You pay by the click or by audience size, and your media planning agency takes a cut. To this chain, add the rich-media vendors, ad networks and media companies and we have a vast and growing paid media ecosystem.

But we're not going to be able to call it "paid media" much longer. Interactive display advertising, on which an agency earns a commission that is a percentage of the banner space buy, is morphing into new forms of "message delivery" in which there is no media spending and, hence, no agency commissions.

Michael Rosenfeld, New Business Director at Mediasmith, deals with this new world on a daily basis.

Michael tells us that marketers are not only looking for success with traditional branding vehicles such as online display advertising, and direct response vehicles like search, but are also asking questions like the following:

- Are widgets relevant and should we make one?

- Should we advertise on social networking sites or build a profile on Facebook?

- How can we effectively seed video?

- How can we make something viral?

- How effective is in-text advertising when coupled with display and search?

- Is it worth making expensive rich-media display ads?

- When ad inventory is low, how do we reach our audience?

Rosenfeld notes that there is no cookie cutter approach. "One of the first things any marketer needs to do is really define who their audience is. Once a target has been appropriately identified you need to research *how* the target and subtargets are consuming media—paid and non-paid." Before buying any media, a marketer should know what sites the target audience is likely to visit, whether they are busily interacting on social networks, and if and where they read blogs, watch web videos and participate in virtual worlds.

So many of these newer advertising opportunities involve media that is not "paid" in the traditional sense. While some enterprises can and do wade out on their own, with shoestring budgets and a lot of patience, into the plummy depths or stinking pools of Web 2.0 communities, most organizations realize the learning curve is much faster if you outsource to a smart and web-savvy agency. Smart agencies are also experimenting with how to charge for message delivery, which means that negotiating a good price may be well within the reach of all organizations, large and small.

Paid media for the purposes of this chapter includes:

- Paid search for placements and rankings on search engines.

- Banner advertisements purchased on individual websites or through ad networks.

- Contextual web ads (i.e., Google AdSense), which are essentially small display ads that appear during an Internet search.

- Sponsorships that include branded opportunities on social networks, nonprofits, and strategic partner websites.

About 45 percent of Internet ad spending today goes to paid search. The remainder pays for a mix of paid media, including banners, rich media, ad networks, sponsorships, blogs, widgets and gadgets and web video ads. Web video ads were discussed in Chapter 6 and blogs in Chapter 8. All of the others will be covered in this chapter.

AD SERVER PLATFORMS: THE NEW MIDDLEMEN

Third-party ad serving is a vital function that distributes ads, records clicks and supports the online ad ecosystem. They are so vital that Microsoft and Google each saw the necessity of buying one of the two largest ad-serving companies.

Google bought DoubleClick, whose DART for Publishers shares the DART platform with DART for Advertisers, as well as with a host of other products. Microsoft bought Aquantive, parent of Atlas, the other leading ad server, which has a similar suite of products.

Ad servers don't only place ads on sites, they also count them, choose the ads that will make the website or advertiser the most money and monitor results of multiple campaigns. They can upload "traditional" banners as well as rich media and have the intelligence to traffic ads according to business rules, to target groups of users and to optimize based upon defined results. In addition they generate enormous amounts of data on user behavior like impressions, clicks and postimpression activity.

Automated functionality may include:

- *Roadblocks*—displaying ads so an advertiser can own 100 percent of the ad inventory on a page. (On a home page, this is called a "home-page takeover.")
- *Exclusion*—excluding competitive ads so users do not see competitors' ads directly next to one another. Also known as blacklisting.

- *Frequency capping*—making sure users only see messages a limited amount of times.

- *Surround sessions*—sequencing ads so users see messages in a specific order.

- *Behavioral targeting*—using prior behavior to determine which ad to show a viewer during a visit. For example, targeting video game ads on a portal to a viewer who was known to have visited a gamer site.

- *Contextual targeting*—determining the optimum ad placement from information contained on the page where the ad is being served. For example, placing snowboard ads automatically on a page with a snowboarding article.

- *Creative optimization*—using predictive modeling to determine the optimal creative for a given ad.

AD PURCHASE METHODOLOGIES

The three most common ways in which online advertising is purchased are CPM, CPC, and CPA.

- *CPM (cost per impression)*—advertisers pay for exposure of their message to a specific audience. Derived from print advertising, the web CPM costs are priced per thousand web page impressions.

- *CPC (cost per click), also known as PPC (pay per click)*—advertisers pay every time a user clicks on their ad and is redirected to their website or landing page. They only pay when the ad is clicked on.

- *CPA (cost per action or cost per acquisition)*—performance-based advertising in which the publisher takes all the risk of running the ad, and the advertiser pays only for the number of users who complete a transaction, such as a purchase or sign-up.

In any of these scenarios, it is important to target an acceptable *cost per conversion,* with the definition of "conversion" varying depending on the situation: it may be a lead, a sale, a download or a trial use. The cost per conversion is calculated by dividing the total cost of an ad campaign by the number of conversions.

Marketers are beginning to view the alternate channels of blogs, social networks, and virtual worlds in terms of reach and frequency. In the offline world, *reach* is how many different people are exposed to a particular ad at least once during a four-week period while *frequency* is how many times someone has been exposed to the ad during the four weeks. Only relatively recently are planning tools and data sources applying the valuable concepts of reach and frequency to online planning.

A whack on the head for many was that buying banner advertisements and web video commercials on social networks, such as MySpace and Facebook, was starting to look like a tremendous waste of time and money. Unlike search.

The reason was obvious. Someone who is using a computer for search wants to click into a website that may fill a need. They are ready to be sold, convinced or at least open to a message that is relevant to their search.

Social network users log on to meet new people, chat with friends and flirt. Most of the time, they're not in buying mode, no matter what you're selling. As Joshua Porter put it in his much-discussed blog posting, "Why Social Ads Don't Work" (bokardo.com/tag/facebook/): "Imagine if every time you talked with your friends they were trying to sell you something. They wouldn't last long as your friend."

Early experiments in advertising on virtual worlds were equally dismal. The Second Life universe is littered with "islands" and "storefronts" purchased by major corporations and then abandoned. In Second Life, participants want to interact with each other and flirt even more, and they'll use their Lindens (currency in Second Life) to purchase larger-than-life-size genitalia for their online avatar. They're not interested in finding out products for their mundane real lives.

But, some forms of paid advertising do work in social media. These include sponsorships and branded entertainment. Games, quizzes, puzzles and treasure hunts that involve off-line activities (such as watching TV programs or going to a live concert) work well. Dell recently had a successful campaign on Facebook, created by Federated Media, that centered around a drawing contest (see www.chasnote.com/2008/02/01/dell-goes-green-1000000-votes-for-dell/) to rebrand the computer company as an environmentally sensitive supporter of the planet.

As you've heard before, the Internet is a "tell me, don't sell me" medium. The Dell logo on the Facebook page disappeared within minutes of page loading, but the campaign took in more than 7,000 entries to the contest, and received coverage throughout the web, including about 2,000 blog sites.

Plastering sales messages in a social environment won't work because it misses the key premise of successful online marketing that Dell understands: *engagement*.

THE BUILDING BLOCKS OF ONLINE PAID MEDIA

The elements of online paid media are familiar to many. What's changing now are the ways in which these familiar formats can be more aggressive and successful when they are truly targeted through new analytical tools.

Banners

Banners are display ads embedded in web pages. Banners come in various sizes. The sizes have names like "skyscrapers" (long verticals) and "leaderboards" (skinny horizontals). Usually the ads are delivered to content sites by third-party ad-serving companies like DoubleClick and Atlas. Advertisers buy banners on a CPM basis. When the banner is loaded into a user's browser, an impression is recorded and the advertiser pays the website. When a user clicks the ad, a click-through is recorded.

Banners got a bad rap in the past because click-through rates of banner ads at one time dipped to below 0.001, largely due to their proliferation and general cheesiness. Today it is more widely accepted that a banner plays a more important role in branding online than it does in direct sales, and so has value in the media mix.

Banner ads appear on blog sites and some social networking sites, and can either be purchased or placed on the websites of your affiliates or business partners. Your banner buys can be highly segmented or web-wide.

Specialty agencies abound. Federated Media allows you to pick among a variety of sports or technology blogs to attract a young demographic and custom-tune your targeting to a single site or dozens. Large

Figure 9-2 Federated Media's buy-it-yourself page

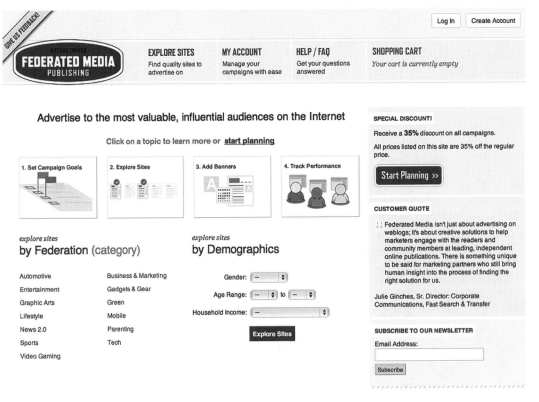

publishers such as Time Warner offer "run of web" that allow you to purchase banner ad space on hundreds of websites within its online network.

In the middle are hundreds of entrepreneurial web publishers with strings of demographically appealing websites with highly flexible rate cards that cater to women, men, mothers, fathers, fast food junkies, gourmands and virtually any other niche group of enthusiasts you can imagine. Some examples: Gawker.com and Sugar (sugarinc.com).

Supporting technologies enable "rich" media display, essentially multimedia creations in which pictorial elements move, expand or explode, all in an effort to get your attention.

Standard Banner and Skyscraper Sizes (measurements shown in pixels)

- Sizes for banner/button ads
  - Full banner: 468 by 60
  - Half banner: 234 by 60
  - Micro button: 80 by 15
  - Micro bar: 88 by 31
  - Button 1: 120 by 90
  - Button 2: 120 by 60
  - Vertical banner: 120 by 240
  - Square button: 125 square
  - Leaderboard: 728 by 90
- Sizes for skyscraper ads
  - Wide skyscraper: 160 by 600
  - Skyscraper: 120 by 600
  - Half-page ad: 300 by 600

Interstitials

Interstitials are ads that load between two content pages. While some interstitials are pop-up ads (see below), others are full pages that interrupt the sequence and force the user to view the ad before continuing to the nest content. Users often find these annoying and search for the (usually very small) "close" button. They, however, can be very effective in garnering user attention and can be appropriate for branding campaigns.

Pop-Ups and Pop-Unders

An annoying and discredited ad format is the pop-up and its relative, the pop-under. These annoying things either appear on top of what you are reading and hover (the pop-up) or appear similarly when a window is closed (the pop-under). These are so annoying that most reputable advertisers refrain from them. They are, however, effective and therefore are still out there. The fact that pop-up blockers have been built into browsers is one of the reasons these annoying ad units are in decline, as well.

Other Flavors of Display Advertising

Widgets and video ads are forms of paid media, discussed in other chapters. An interesting alternative to banners is a monetization experiment used for The Million Dollar Home Page (www.themilliondollarhomepage.com) in which visitors/advertisers bought individual pixels of the page for a dollar.

Rich Media

Rich media, usually utilizing Adobe Flash, turns banners into multimedia units that can expand and explode. They have come to prominence because they are effective, although they are usually more expensive to produce, and it certainly takes longer to design and code a banner that may have several moving parts. Movement and sound engage user attention, and increase conversion rates. Rich media allows web users to "play" on a screen, mousing over sections of an ad that can then be clicked through to specific destinations related to the user's area of interest. Highly popular in automotive, packaged goods and finance, rich media ads can include music clips and video.

Here are some of the typical rich media executions:

- Floating ad—moves across the user's screen or floats above the content.
- Expanding ad—changes size and which may alter the contents of the webpage.
- Polite ad—a large ad will be downloaded in smaller pieces to minimize the disruption of the content being viewed
- Wallpaper ad—changes the background of the page being viewed.
- Map ad—text or graphics linked from, and appearing in or over, a location on an electronic map such as Google Maps.
- Streaming ad—containing streaming audio or video.

Aside from the expense, the other caveat for rich media ads is to optimize them for the very small screen, for the cell phone display as well as PDA. Figure in additional budget for this coding and perhaps new creative. The reality is this: if you've got time and a talented teenager who knows how to use Flash, the cost can be nothing. If you're an agency with a car account, you will bill out $20,000 in design costs for essentially the same animation.

These multimedia banner ads can catch your eye with blazing innovation, but they don't have to. In some cases, a good static banner that states your message clearly will outperform one that whirls around and whistles Dixie.

What makes a banner pull? Here are a few suggestions. Think less text, more picture. Strong visual images that resonate with your target audience are powerful. We sometimes wonder why web advertisers don't avail themselves of the same richness of image they employ so well in print ads, now that high-speed connections and broadband make sharp, clear visuals possible on all screens. And in any global marketplace, good art pushes past language barriers and gets your message across in that fraction of a second you have to capture your international audience.

Don't sell in the banner, tell in the banner. As mentioned in the previous chapter, Edward Lamoureaux of West Glen Communications in New York has found substantial success incorporating public relations messaging into the text of banner ads. For example, instead of saying "Click Here to Support Breast Cancer Research," the message could read, "If you or someone you know has breast cancer, watch this video."

CONTEXTUAL ADVERTISING

Google and Yahoo!, among others, have harnessed their search technology to enable the serving of a context-triggered ad on content websites. They have created networks of content sites and now allow advertisers to deselect specific sites. This is sometimes considered a kind of search, simply because it is the large search companies that have used their technology to dominate the market. In particular, Google's AdSense product has the largest market share for this type of advertising. But, in truth, this is just another form of display advertising. Adjacency to relevant content has always been among the goals of display in print and on the web, and the contextual networks simply automate the process.

Google AdSense relies on keyword purchase (as in enquiry search) to trigger ad display.

Contextual ads rarely have conversion rates as good as enquiry search, as they are not responding to a purchase intent.

Another paid media product is embedding keyword hyperlinks in an article that are sponsored by an advertiser. When a user follows the link, they are sent to a sponsor's website. Vibrant (VibrantMedia.com) is a leading purveyor of this technology.

SPONSORSHIPS AND BRANDED ENTERTAINMENT

Sponsored content, like "brought to you by" radio, can buy familiarity, if not loyalty, among web users. Live streaming performances, web video programming, live chat forums, contests and sweepstakes can all be sponsored as a part of your offline and online media mix. Charity auctions, sign-up campaigns for world relief or local causes, silly surveys and invitations to submit reviews, photographs, opinions and general venting can all be sponsored on your website, on the sites of strategic partners, content sites and social networking sites.

Pass-alongs to "friends" can move your message faster in social networking sites. Add a widget application that can be posted on a personal page, blog or sent by email to another person. Now, your audience is your ad server network. Though harder to track and impossible to control, the exposure is free and helps extend the dollars you spend.

CASE STUDY: Napster Returns

Mediasmith's work with Napster involved an awareness strategy for launch that could later feed into a direct response strategy. The ultimate goal was to obtain two-week trial users who were likely to convert to subscribers of a pay-for-music-download service that hoped to replicate the success of its previous incarnation, a free (and highly illegal) file sharing platform for MP3 music downloads. Reducing the cost of acquiring each trial participant was also a factor.

Believing that fresh creative was essential to meeting these goals, the agency advocated that Napster's in-house creative team come up with two or three versions of each of ten different concepts, with new executions always ready in the queue. Thus armed with an array of sufficient creative resources, Mediasmith crafted a hybrid strategy that combined email, guerrilla marketing, out-of-home advertising (billboards, posters, street flyers), web advertising and search.

Derek Leedy, VP of Client Services, notes that the campaign began with scrubbing the Napster legacy email database, which had been dormant for several years while Napster worked its way through the copyright courts. The scrub took the list down from 10 million emails to 3 million good emails. That list of verified emails was the first place they reached out to, reconnecting with potential Napster loyalists. They then did vignettes featuring the Napster kitty escaping from jail, proclaiming that Napster was back. Seven episodes later, a buzz had started.

Several weeks before the launch, out-of-home wild postings were used creatively. Posters of a fictitious event were posted and then were "defaced" by being covered with images of the Napster cat.

Online and print display ads were run in music publications and on websites. A faux "wild man" was even employed to display a "Napster Is Coming Back" sign. Complex flash ads were created treating the Napster brand in edgy ways. Dance club promotions were executed with special "Napster Nights." Athletes like BMX racer Ryan Nyquist were recruited to endorse Napster.

All these brand- and buzz-building activities eventually culminated with print ads in publications like *Time*, and massive web "roadblocks" on sites like Rolling Stone, ESPN and Artist Direct. The ad units included rich media executions with the Napster kitty spitting flame.

For one of the first times a web ad campaign became a TV campaign, when a web execution (showing the Napster kitty, with the voice-over "It's back") was converted directly to a TV commercial.

Figure 9-3 The Napster kitty first appears offline

The campaign had the challenge of explaining Napster's new subscription music model. One way this was accomplished was with a Super Bowl ad urging viewers to compare the cost of a Napster subscription versus buying individual iTunes songs, with the call to action "Do the Math."

The direct response portion of the campaign heavily used CPA ad networks, such as Advertising.com, to drive massive numbers of impressions. The buys were relentlessly optimized to the point that the cost of a trailer had been reduced to less than one quarter of the client's original cost.

Challenge 1: Target definition and development—reintroduce the kitty to the paying community
Reintroducing the music industry's baddest kitty as a legal music downloading pay-service had to take into account that both music downloads

Figure 9-4 This web ad later became a television commercial

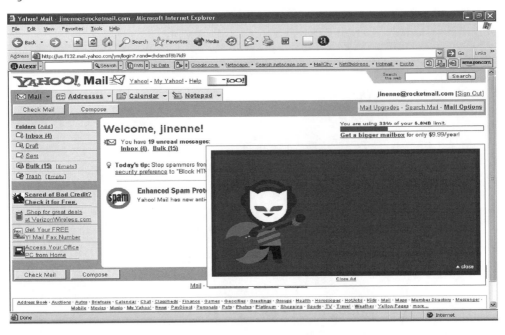

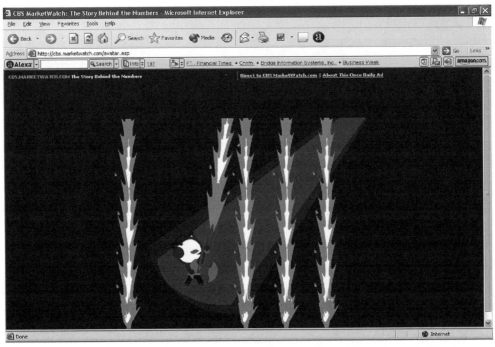

and the target audience of young men had changed. Through research in the target development phase, true targets were identified; this in fact changed the target audience from the preconceived "male 16–22" category and moved the crosshair to the "adult 25–44 music lover" who is technologically proficient and has extra money to spend.

While males between the ages of 16 and 22 are heavy music downloaders, they are also (still) heavily into illegal file-sharing. Mediasmith analyzed and developed a universe of conceivable new customers, based on a number of different data sources, and found the more likely target to be adults (men and women alike) between the ages of 25 and 44 who have an affinity to music, are technologically proficient, and are willing and able to place a recurring charge on their credit card. That this group included women as well as men meant a broader brush for both online and offline design.

Challenge 2: Reach, frequency, and engagement—while competing with iTunes
With a limited budget (compared to Apple) and huge expectations, Napster needed a campaign that announced its triumphant return without over-hyping or otherwise hurting its credibility.

Having established the new target audience, Mediasmith developed a complex integrated media campaign focusing on the new target's media habits. This included print (15 magazines), broadcast (season openers and series premiers), online (takeovers, roadblocks, eyeBlaster rich media), search (SEO/SEM), and out-of-home actions (Guerilla street teams, car wraps, billboards, wild postings and a Jumbotron impression or two).

Napster knew it was outspent and so it relied on a veteran agency's strengths, getting face time for a media campaign around music, lifestyle, technology, news and sports. Leveraging extensive senior contacts in the media community and years of buying power, Mediasmith pulled 15 magazines with 27 covers in four months. The TV ads aired on the season premier of *South Park* as well as a number of key, proven audience drivers such as

LeBron James's regular rookie year season NBA games. The campaign dove deep into highly trafficked websites using a variety of rich media creative, and outdoor efforts were presented in six major metros where wild postings, billboards, videotrons, projection videos and a handful of Napster-branded Mini Coopers rolled the streets straight out of *The Italian Job*.

Challenge 3: Metrics on the fly
With so many elements in play, delivering impressions through different channels, the campaign needed to track, report and optimize around the clock.

Here are the very impressive final numbers:

- The online, print, broadcast and guerilla campaign achieved a 95.5 percent reach for the strategic target audience with an average frequency of 8.6.
- Using a mixed approach, 24 percent was allocated toward interactive. This provided greater efficiency in the plan and enabled Napster to move the acquisition cost per trial user from $144 to $22.
- With these efficiencies, Mediasmith saved 44 percent across a $3 million print plan.

METRICS AND MEASUREMENT

Direct Marketing on Steroids

> In a perfectly behavioral-targeted world, if you never saw a Mercedes ad until you could afford one and were ready to purchase, *how would you know you wanted a Mercedes?* Shouldn't you have aspired to that brand long before you walked into the dealership? If not, we've essentially decided that brand building is irrelevant. And I don't think we really want to go there.
>
> **—JOSH CHASIN (*METRICS INSIDER*, JANUARY 22, 2008)**

For most marketers, there is only one metric that counts: conversions. This usually means sales—how many sales did the banner ad or that email blast bring in? How many newsletter sign-ups or web video pass-alongs were created in a MySpace campaign?

Out of ignorance or laziness, that's usually about as far as most executives get when it comes to exploring better ways to improve their online operations.

Enterprises launching new or updated websites may obsess about the following as well:

- Search engine rankings (how far up on a search page the website appears).

- Unique visitors (how many users visit your website per day, week or month).

- Page views (how many web pages did web users visit within your site).

- "Stickiness" (how much time did users spend on your site?), also known as duration or engagement.

These all provide clues but they are not the whole picture, and they can all be misleading.

Let's take the "unique visitor" metric, for example. Every visitor to a website, from the accidental keyboarder who hits the site and clicks away a few seconds later, to the frequent participant who spends an hour each day perusing the site, are counted the same way—once. But these visitors are not alike. Teenagers who surf on line, watch TV and talk to their friends at the same time are not necessarily as engaged with the brand as another young visitor who arrives via a blog link, downloads a game or a recording, then moves on.

Stickiness is also suspect. Efficient websites may be penalized in this metric if their navigation is so good that customers can arrive online, make a purchase and move on. Many direct marketers such as LL Bean and Land's End use a "Quick Shop" menu to direct customers quickly to a purple sports shirt they may have seen in a catalog when they key in a SKU number. Is this experience inferior to having customers burn minutes looping through hierarchal menus of product descriptions? We think not.

MEASUREMENT AND RATINGS: WHO COUNTS? WHO CARES?

Just as television and radio have their ratings services, and magazines and print have their verification watchdogs, a few leaders in the industry are relied on for ratings. This doesn't mean they count clicks: many ratings seen in trade press are the product of audience surveys, polls, panels and metering systems, rather than hard numbers.

The comScore Global Network is the largest continuously measured consumer panel of its kind. Their unified system collects and reports the information needed to support smarter decisions for a variety of business functions, including market and competitive research, media planning and analysis, segmentation analysis, market testing, attitudinal surveys and financial analysis. A comScore rating looks a little deeper into a visitor's overall website experience, with the number of return visits, the amount of time spent on site and the total number of internal page views per visit all factors in rating.

Nielsen Online, by comparison, recently shifted its key metrics components away from page views and into time spent on a site as a ratings marker. This service delivers comprehensive, independent measurement and analysis of online audiences, advertising, video, consumer-generated media, word of mouth, commerce and consumer behavior, and includes products previously marketed under the Nielsen//NetRatings and Nielsen BuzzMetrics brands, which operate under the BuzzMetricsNielsen Online unit within The Nielsen Company, well known for its work in broadcast TV audience measurement with black box meters in the home.

In 2009, Nielsen hopes to have meters on home computers as well, to measure the amount of time spent watching television programs and other video content on the web. Advertisers would be able to discover, for example, how many viewers watched the television episode on a video channel such as veoh.com, or only watched a snippet of the program that did not include a commercial break.

Quantcast is a new media measurement service that enables advertisers to view audience reports for millions of sites and services to build their brands with confidence. The free service empowers publishers to demonstrate the unique value of their audiences by tagging their websites, videos, widgets and games for direct measurement. Still, it relies on a census rather than a survey.

Quantcast doesn't put much weight on duration, but it does count visitors by how often they return to a site. As a measurement of loyalty this may have some weight with advertisers looking to establish brand relationships with specific websites.

Because these and other online rating services often disagree when counting website data, the trade groups Web Analytics Association and the Internet Advertising Bureau have been earnestly looking into standardization of key metrics, such as a page view.

BENCHMARKS

Your site reports, often referred to as server logs, provides all the data you need to see how many people are visiting your website, what kinds of activities they do there, and where they have been referred from other points on the Internet. Traffic patterns in and out of your site can help measure campaign effectiveness. Traffic numbers, along with the number of page impressions served and the number of unique visitors, are critical if you plan to monetize your site by selling advertising space.

To get an idea of how far you may go, these were the most visited websites in the fourth quarter of 2007:

News portals, which are highly trafficked, highly searched and sell premium ad space fiercely compete for traffic levels. While you may not be a direct competitor with a news organization, on any day a major news story breaks your own traffic levels may take a steep drop. News portals are generally better for brand building than for direct marketing or a conversion-centric campaign, due to the difficulty of measuring the precise demographics of their readership.

Figure 10-1 Most highly rated websites, December 2007.

Top 20 Parent Companies at Home and Work, December 2007		
Parent	Unique Audience (000)	Time Per Person (hr:min:sec)
Google	124,631	1:38:56
Microsoft	123,208	2:08:22
Yahoo	114,148	3:05:35
Time Warner	106,277	3:45:47
News Corp. Online	76,325	2:01:46
eBay	67,443	1:59:03
Amazon	65,438	0:35:57
InterActiveCorp	64,141	0:23:56
Apple Computer	50,686	1:15:10
Wikimedia Foundation	50,474	0:15:39
New York Times Co.	48,718	0:17:33
Walt Disney Internet Group	45,647	0:36:55
E.W. Scripps Co.	43,189	0:09:00
AT&T Inc.	43,156	0:36:27
Landmark Communications	41,998	0:22:46
Wal-Mart Stores	39,513	0:18:09
Target Corp.	38,026	0:09:30
RealNetworks Inc.	37,262	0:41:55
CNET Networks	34,915	0:10:32
Office Max	30,121	0:07:26

Source: Nielsen Online, 2008

Figure 10-2 A sampling of top news sites

MEASURING PERFORMANCE IN A PAY-FOR-PERFORMANCE UNIVERSE

If you're using paid media, your site report and the reports generated by your third-party ad server may not be enough to adequately measure the return on investments made in online display ads, search and email campaigns. A great many marketers who are bullish on paid search always point to successful conversion rates. But these also may be misleading. This may be especially damaging for organizations that, in a recessionary economy, may have to dial down the dollars they spend on online marketing. Sticking to what seems to have worked in the past may be a losing strategy.

The "Last Click" Controversy

Those marketers tempted to go the less expensive route and just purchase search rather than bother with display advertising may be sacrificing more than lift—they may lose the whole ballgame. That's what Brian McAndrews is telling us.

And Brian McAndrews isn't just anybody. He's the former CEO of aQuantive and is now a Microsoft senior vice president in charge of competing with other engines for ad dollars. So we should pay attention.

McAndrews says search is given too much credit because of the way the effectiveness of ads is measured. When an online transaction takes place, the sale is attributed to the last ad viewed, which is most often a search ad.

"Since search logically is often the last thing people do, it's arguably getting more credit than it deserves," he said. "It's probably being overvalued now. Our studies show that it is." He cites as an example, if a customer sees a banner promoting a product on Microsoft's MSN and watches a related video on Time Warner Inc.'s AOL and then searches for the brand on Google before making a purchase, only Google gets credit for the sale.

At recent search conferences there has been much discussion of the "last click" issue, with conjecture that each industry might have its own formula for weighting "assists" that lead to a conversion. Most agreed that the "last click" has been overattributed, in general to the benefit of Google.

Until very recently, neither Atlas (part of aQuantive, now Microsoft) nor DoubleClick (now a part of Google) could "see beyond the last click" to show the role of display ads and other search terms in contributing to the "final click." Now, Atlas, DoubleClick, Eyeblaster and others offer tags such as Atlas's Universal Action Tag that reveal the path the user took to get to a conversion. It's this newly available data, McAndrews argues, that will diminish the relative importance of search and boost other kinds of online advertising.

Beyond the new tags, McAndrews said Microsoft is working on a system called "conversion attribution" that would dole out credit to other sources that influenced the buyer's decision. He expects that system to replace the current one, which was originally developed by aQuantive. The implication is that this system would reduce the importance of search.

Since MSN doesn't do as well with search as rivals Google and Yahoo!, this might seem like a case of a Microsoft fox souring on a competitor's grape. But Dave Smith of Mediasmith recently brought back a great case study from his travels to Australia that seems to illustrate McAndrews's thesis.

This is from a case study example provided by Australian agency dgm (www.dgm-au.com) at the iMedia Agency Summit in Hunter Valley, Australia. The client had a search effort garnering 3,000 customers a month at a $40 CPA. They had 1,000 customers from web banner advertising at a $130 CPA. Other efforts like affiliate and email had a $60–90 CPA, garnering 2,300 customers a month. The client directed the agency to cut the "expensive" web CPA sites. The agency did so, getting it down to $100. The 1,000 customers dropped to 650. The 2,300 dropped to 2,080. The 3,000 in search dropped to 2,250. Overall volume dropped by 21 percent.

Net, net: Web banners, even though they had a higher CPA, enabled the overall scaling of a campaign to higher volume. When they took away key sites that contributed to the branding of the advertising, fewer people knew about the offer, and fewer went to search.

This does not diminish the importance of search marketing, but it is more likely to enable us to really see the interrelationships of media exposure and to plan accordingly. Our old colleague Rick Bruner (with DoubleClick, and now with Google) and John Chandler of Atlas recently teamed up for a presentation on "attribution management" that could be shown to track how adding display lifted conversions by 22 percent even though about 70 percent of the "final clicks" came directly from search links.

Simple Tools for the Bootstrapper

- *Adbutler (Adbutler.com):* This is an inexpensive "training wheels" banner management and tracking system that counts IBM, Compaq, Boeing, Merrill Lynch, Toshiba, the *New York Times* and the *Washington Post* among its client base. In exchange for a percentage of ad space in rotation (currently 7.5 percent) the service is free, while a premium paid service includes a wide range of reporting functions and customer support.

- *Linkpopularity.com:* This is an old favorite free service that still works. Simply type in the name of your website (or your competitor's) and the engine will return the number of links the site has on Google, Yahoo! and MSN. Clicking onto the server names brings up the links to view which news sites, blogs or future strategic partners are linking in.

- *Hit counters:* Also called site meters. A variety of free counters for the smaller enterprise are available, including "invisible" meters that count stats for you but don't reveal your startup's pathetic four-figure stats. Check out statcounter.com or search for "hit counter" online. Most professional marketers, and more importantly, professional advertisers, see hit tachometers on a site and immediately think "amateur," so don't fall into some vanity trap that will only dissuade the pros from working with you.

ANALYTICS SOFTWARE VENDORS FOR THE ENTERPRISE

Not surprisingly, a variety of vendors provide highly sophisticated software—web analytics tools—that generate reports of all sorts of useful data. These automated systems can help you catch patterns, catch errors and optimize not only your website but email campaigns as well. Web analytics programs use data collected directly from site activity in real time. The data collection can be done on the client side—you supply a counter tool by tagging a page with Javascript or collect data from your host ISP server logs. Or the data collection can be done through an ad-server platform.

Software vendors and service companies supplying analytics tools include WebTrends, CoreMetrics, Unica, Visual Sciences, Omniture and Google. Google Analytics is a great service that is offered free of charge to participants in Google Adwords programs. Since you will most likely be running paid search campaigns on Google, the benefit of completely tracking your keywords in Google Analytics makes the service even more powerful.

Usually, data from an analytics program can be imported to Excel spreadsheets and otherwise translate into plain English for nontechnical staff. Or it may be displayable in visuals such as charts, graphs and meters on a "dashboard" widget that allows a marketer to monitor site activity and conversions in real time, over the course of a day or over the course of a particular campaign.

WHY EVEN GOOD NUMBERS LIE

A very interesting research project done in summer 2007 by Jim Sterne of Stone Temple Consulting (archived at_www.stonetemple.com/articles/analytics-report-august-2007.shtml) compared different web analytics tools on the same set of websites. The test looked at four different websites with analytics tools supplied by ClickTracks, Google Analytics, IndexTools, Unica Affinium's NetInsight, Visual Science's HBX Analytics, Omniture's SiteCatalyst and Web Trends. With the exception of the last two, engineering support was provided by the tools' developers to assist in the test. The results: different tools installed on the same website produce different numbers. In

Figure 10-3 A dashboard utility that tracks web activity

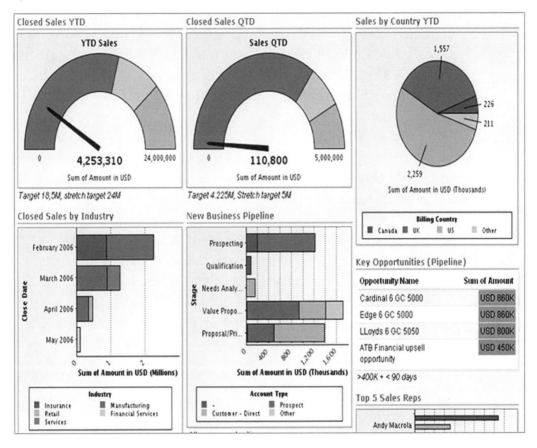

some cases the variance was staggering, as high as a 150 percent difference, according to Sterne.

A few factors cropped up to explain the variances. One involved the use of JavaScript on the site; if placed low on a screen page (below the fold, you might say) a slow load might result in some visitors leaving the page before the JavaScript program could be executed. Thus, the data for that visit would be lost, and data regarding the original landing page, as well as keyword data (if the visitor came in from a search engine) would not be recorded or counted.

Time lag in counting also made a difference. In the test, it was observed that sometimes Google counted more, but generally counted
faster. The Google tool executed its count in an average speed of 0.07
seconds, while the next closest, IndexTools, took 4 seconds to execute
the count. The differential of 3.3 seconds may be significant considering it takes much less time for a web user to click onto a web page, look
around and depart.

Yet another variable was the use of cookies, or more specifically,
their disabling by users. Cookie blocking and cookie deletion by users
(particularly third-party cookies) was found to alter traffic levels by
about 15 to 20 percent. To quote Sterne:

> Cookie deletion rates are of great concern when evaluating web analytics. Every
> time a cookie is deleted it impacts the visitor and unique visitor counts of the
> tool. In particular, counting of unique visitors is significantly affected. If a user
> visits a site in the morning, deletes their cookies, and then visits again in the af-
> ternoon, this will show up as two different daily unique visitors in the totals for
> that day, when in fact one user made multiple visits, and should be counted only
> as one unique visitor.

But, he adds, "Even if an analytics package is measuring the behavior of only 80 percent of their users, it remains highly relevant and valuable data. By contrast, the traditional print industry relies on subscriber
surveys, and feels lucky if they get 20 percent response. They would die
for data on 80 percent of their customers."

The study was useful in that it uncovered typical reasons why a metric might not be counted properly. First among them: tagging errors.
Making mistakes in placing JavaScript on a web page turns out to be a
common problem when every page has to be tagged, and whenever
pages are updated, added or removed.

"One way to reduce many of these risks is to install multiple analytics packages," Sterne noted. "We often put Google Analytics on sites,
even if they already have an analytics package on them. This is not to

say that Google Analytics is the gold standard. With this approach, however, if you spot substantial differences (30 percent or more, for example) between the two packages, that would provide you a visible clue that something may have gone wrong in your tagging or setup."

METRICS FOR WEB 2.0: COUNTING WIDGETS, VIRAL VIDEOS, LOYALTY AND ENGAGEMENT

Keeping track of viral programming can be easier if materials are tagged before sent off into the World Wide Web. This helps tracking, but analyzing the data is still rather vague.

Jodi McDermott is one of several web gurus proposing that measuring the effectiveness of a widget can be quantified, by combining three types of data—the number of times a widget is imported into a new URL environment ("placements") plus the number of requests to view a widget ("views), divided by the number of unique visitors to the website ("unique visitors").

Viral videos can also be tracked by tagging their URLs with a bit of extra code, which is a method favored by viral consultants like Dan Greenberg.

A loyalty index may provide some measurement of how engaged unique visitors are with a branded website. One clue to this may be return rate. David Smith of Mediasmith recently compared two high-volume websites, the networking site Facebook, and a pure news-and-information site, About.com. In the time period measured, Smith noted that more than 60 percent of Facebook users were returning to the site more than 30 times in a month, or at least once a day, while just 2 percent of About.com's visitors came back on a daily basis.

Again, this doesn't tell the whole story. The statistics suggest that the other 98 percent of About.com visitors presumably found their answer to their specific question and didn't need to come back to the site. And the frequent visitors to the Facebook site may have simply been bored post-teens briefly checking their status on a cell phone, rather than active participants in the online social whirl. Duration data might help here, but that still doesn't quantify how satisfied visitors to either site might feel about the experience.

Eric Peterson is one of several people contemplating how best to measure engagement with a purely statistical analysis. His formula includes some new and interesting metrics that appear to resemble those used to quantify search engine rankings, and include "click depth" as a measure of how many visitors move beyond, say, the first two or three pages of a website, and "recency" as a measure of repeat visitors within a given time frame.

We find this intriguing so we reproduce it (with permission) here:

The Mathematics of Engagement

Click depth (content clicked on): Percentage of visitors who exceed average page views in a given content category. If 26 percent of visitors exceed, say, 3 page views, **C = 26%.**

Loyalty (number of return visits over a longer period of time—say 12 months) [A variable whose weight may be adjusted: for example, a business customer who renews orders on a quarterly basis might be given an **L = 4%**, or perhaps given a higher ratio if his or her past purchase volume was considerably higher than other customers who also purchased quarterly.]

Recency (number of return visits over a shorter period of time, say 1 month): If 5 percent of visitors return more than once a month, **R = 5%.**

Duration (time of session): If a category of content sites records a 4.6-minute average session time and 19 percent of a specific site's visitors spend more than 4.6 minutes, then **D = 19%** for that site.

Interactivity (defined actions taken with content-downloading, posting, attending a video or audiocast, etc): If 32 percent of visitors take any one of these actions, **I = 32%**, during a specified time period.

Subscription (commitment of name and business or personal info): Measures the percentage of visitors who have given registration information. If 21 percent of a site's traffic can be identified by name and other submitted information, then **S = 21%**.

The Total Engagement Index is arrived by adding the values for each engagement category and dividing by 6.

Another metric worth keeping an eye on is the WOM, or word-of-mouth unit. This has proved useful in quantifying the branding effects of viral campaigns and we like its simplicity: 4 WOMs equal one conversion.

KEEPING AN EYE ON ROI

Long-term measurement, from a ROI perspective, is to try to gauge customer (or patron, if you're a nonprofit) acquisition costs. This can be measured in sales units—or against the expected lifetime value of that customer to your organization.

The benefit to this is that what may seem like a big expense online ($100,000 for a branding banner campaign) can be spread out over a year's worth of results. And what may seem to be a bargain $2.00 per click search program turns out to be a nightmare if 50,000 unqualified leads click through and depart without buying a thing.

Online marketers love giveaways. "Free" draws crowds but a premium with a tangible value that relates to your offerings works better. Banks will routinely offer $50 or even $100 to open an online checking or savings account because acquiring new customer assets pays off in the long run. Amazon.com and LLBean.com can offer free shipping during holiday periods because this attracts customers who are on the edge of purchase. Their volume of sales and simple knowledge of human behavior assures that enough will miss the cutoff anyway, and wind up having to pay extra charges to get the gift items there in time for Christmas.

In holiday 2007, analysts did find that online retailers had extraordinary sales—but that profits were hurt by merchants eating the shipping charges. For smaller enterprises, this is where testing shows its value. As does tracking human behaviors on your own site.

Hellotraveler.com is run by Deborah Busch as a commerce site that marries the trend of scrapbooking to international travel, selling photo albums, journals, photo frames and other memory aids. The site offers five different shipping choices—two express and three via U.S Mail. If a customer chooses none, the default is old-fashioned Parcel Post.

Experimenting with email campaigns, Busch compared three offers: one offered free shipping, while the others offered discounts of 10, 15 and 20 percent off retail prices. Busch found the higher percentage discounts brought in more sales than free shipping. But free shipping beat the 10 percent discount offer, suggesting a threshold for products typically priced $20 or less.

The results were intriguing enough to be included in Marketing Sherpa's 2008 *Wisdom Report*, a popular, annual (and free) compendium of good advice contributed by web marketers (www.marketingsherpa/ wisdom).

"Here's the interesting part, more than 50 percent of the time customers don't bother to hit the 'Check Shipping Rates' button," noted Busch. "They just let the default option go through. It's mystifying to us that with a simple click a customer could make an informed, and, often, cheaper choice. But, it seems about half our customers don't care."

ADWARE AND CLICK FRAUD

Click fraud, sometimes more accurately called "impression fraud," is a big and growing problem that has the potential to undermine CPC (cost per click) advertising.

To understand the threat it is important to understand that click fraud is brought to you by the same malevolent but talented program-

Testing, Testing: Test Those eMails!

We were shocked, shocked, shocked to find that in a Datatran 2007 study of 2,000 email marketers, only 74 percent bothered to test or optimize their email campaigns, and only 65 percent actually took the trouble to measure the effectiveness of their emails on actual sales. This is nuts. On email campaigns and other direct response campaigns, your best defense against an expensive endeavor that tanks is to *test* small populations. Test as many variables as possible, and don't take anything as a given.

Some words of advice: The automated analytics vendors mentioned earlier all have email optimizer tools within their suites, and, for the bootstrapper, many freeware or shareware programs exist to help you test your email variables such as daypart, time to send, header copy and offers.

mers who brought you spam. Just as spammers, through their ability to create networks of "bots" were able to virtually overwhelm email and to render direct email virtually useless as a marketing medium, so too are the very same diabolical fraudsters using even more evolved technology to create phony clicks and even phony registrations. This threatens the entire business model of CPC advertising.

There are several types of click fraud. The original and most benign is known as "competitor fraud." In this instance an overzealous rival repeatedly clicks into a competitor's site to drive up costs. There is also "affiliate click fraud," in which affiliates in commission networks commit fraud (by using robot or manual labor) to unjustly enrich themselves by getting credit for false leads. There is also "syndication" fraud, which is now the most prevalent form of click fraud. In this instance, some sites that are syndication partners of search engines such as Google and Yahoo! defraud both their search engine partners and the advertiser by providing phony clicks.

How big is this problem?

Some say that click fraud accounts for 20 to 30 percent of search engine clicks. However, Google and Yahoo! say that the problem is "negligible," mostly because of built-in safeguards.

We believe that, overall, the figure is between 18 to 20 percent. The problem is worse on the second- and third-tier search engines (such as local search and vertical search) and in contextual search, but is present on the first-tier engines as well. There is a higher likelihood of encountering fraud when using Google and Yahoo!'s syndication options. As much as $1 billion of the $5 billion search marketplace may be due to fraudulent clicks, according to Michael Caruso, CEO of ClickFacts.

Google's own CFO, George Reyes, told an investor's conference that "I think something needs to be done about this [click fraud] really, really quickly, because I think, it potentially threatens our business model." Amazing but true: a California man was caught trying to blackmail Google into paying him $150,000 for his click fraud software, which he threatened to unleash against the search engine giant.

A recent study by SEMPO, an organization of search professionals, suggested that 45 percent of search advertisers were concerned about the issue. A graphic illustration comes from John Squire, chief strategy officer of Coremetrics, who said "click fraud is a fin sticking out of the water; you're not sure if it's a great white shark or a dolphin."

Click Fraud Is International

A recent article in the *Times of India* noted that when you type "earn rupees clicking ads" into Google, you get 25,000 listings. The newspaper highlighted one worker whose job it is to click on online ads. She makes $100 to $200 per day at about 20 cents per click. The paper quotes another as saying "I have no interest in what appears when clicking an ad. I care only whether to pause 60 seconds or 90 seconds, as money is credited if you stay online for a fixed time."

PUZZLING OUT THE METRICS OF ENGAGEMENT: AN INTERVIEW WITH DAVE SMITH

Dave Smith is the founder if Mediasmith and is universally regarded as one of the brightest minds in media. Bob Heyman sat down and discussed digital engagement with him.

BOB: In a recent article, you wrote about engagement, saying that it was more of an effectiveness metric than an exposure metric. What did you mean?

DAVE: Engagement, while related to the medium that carries the message, is primarily a product- or service-oriented attribute. Let me give an example: Opting in is a sign that you are engaged. You have made the decision to get involved with messaging from a brand by agreeing to have it sent to you on a regular basis.

In my mind, engagement is clearly on the shoulders of the brand and those who convey the message. But it is not totally in the control of the messaging (advertising) or the media (publisher) folks. Two examples: while a commercial, print ad, Internet message or some other form might convince me to try a new toothpaste or soap (yep, probably a TV spot, as they still work best for a lot of new things), I probably do not become fully engaged with the product until I try it in the shower, smell it and feel it. Yet I became engaged with the Maserati Gran Turismo Coupe the first time I saw it at an auto show. Engagement is an unconscious tick of the mind that causes you to think differently about and notice a brand differently in the future. And advertising can help big time in this process.

BOB: So where does engagement fit as a metric?

DAVE: While it is clear that engagement is a really cool word to use to describe communication and involvement of the campaign with the consumer, it feels more like

a psychographic word than a metric and its place is not up at the reach and frequency level. As just one example, the Advertising Research Foundation's media
model for communication looks like this:

- Vehicle distribution
- Vehicle exposure
- Advertising exposure
- Advertising attentiveness
- Advertising communication
- Advertising persuasion
- Advertising response
- Sales response

Advertising exposure is the line that reach and frequency reside on. Engagement is probably a good thing to put a little further down the line, but it is not
logical that you can be engaged with an ad unless you have been exposed first. So,
the question is whether engagement belongs with attentiveness, communication,
persuasion or response.

Bob: How is the web working for creating and measuring engagement?

Dave: The web has a clear lead in engagement. After all, did you ever even hear the
term "opt in" before the web came along—even though we had been opting in to
catalogues, consciously or unconsciously, for years? Registrations, downloads, visits
to a site, purchases, requests for more information—you name it. That's why I don't
recommend using the CPA term in computing efficiency. CPA is now forever
branded in the metric associated with an online ad sales methodology. I suggest that
you use CPW—cost-per-whatever you are trying to measure. Once you do this, you
end up having discussions about engagement metrics.

With other media, we evaluate them all based on their CPM, or cost-per-
thousand impressions. With the web—and other media as they become digital and

trackable—the subject changes to CPW, not CPM. And we end up having two discussions. First, what is the "W" that we are going to measure? Then, what kind of CPW can we achieve, and does that meet the goal to successfully sell the product or service at a profit? We're over 10 years into the web advertising revolution, yet none of the other media that we use can measure up to the metrics of the web.

If you want engagement, other media can claim it, but only the web can prove what the cost per engaged user is, whatever your metric.

Bob: How is the ad industry thinking about engagement?

Dave: Interestingly, the AAAA is calling engagement "the new frequency." More than a year ago, before there was much in the way of definition for engagement, I heard Erwin Ephron speak on this topic at OMMA East. Mr. Ephron, who knows more than a little bit about this (some call him the founder of modern media planning), said that we should look inside at our current metrics and information available before we throw everything out and start over. I agree with him. For example, he indicates that we could measure TV through bringing together the following variables: size of the unit, clutter, situation and relevance. It seems, though, that it involves more. And indeed, by examining his ebook of essays, *Engagement Explained (and That's Not Easy),* available from his website (www.ephronmedia.com), Mr. Ephron does agree that more than media must be taken into account. "Media engagement and advertising engagement are very different things." He goes on to say, "Historically, media are measured by audience delivery. Advertising is measured by response. Engagement-based ratings would measure media by response."

It is clear that the context and relevancy of advertising is important. And, the effectiveness of the advertising is such a huge variable that one cannot simply expect that we can develop engagement metrics for the media and be done with it. As Mr. Ephron quotes FCB's Roger Baron: "If you want engagement, make a more engaging ad."

Bob: So how do we evolve an "engagement" metric?

Dave: One thing is clear, the working definition, which is that "engagement is turning on a prospect to a brand idea enhanced by the surrounding content," is not enough.

Bob: So, will engagement be the new reach?

Dave: Doubtful. It cannot be rationalized as the new frequency either. Taking all of the above into account, measuring engagement is a worthy goal and more energy should be spent on the basic definitional stage and the "what does it really mean" stage by industry bodies. While it is fine to measure campaigns at the exposure or OTS [opportunity to see] or phase [impressions, GRPs, reach and frequency], in the end we'd all like a metric that demonstrates that the consumer is "involved" with our advertising and "gets it." Engagement is as good a term as any for this metric, it just has some ways to go before we have a definition we can all live with and execute true metrics behind.

NEW MARKETING CHANNELS

Virtual Worlds, Advergaming and Wireless Mobile Search

Anyone who says TV is dead, hold the phone: there's your TV.

—DAVID MURPHY, PRESIDENT OF SAATCHI & SAATCHI

JUST WHEN YOU THOUGHT you were starting to get your mind around social networks, its time to stretch it to the limit with virtual worlds.
Think of this as being movie sequels run amok. First we had news
groups and bulletin boards all across the web where people of like interests could post and interact. The sequel was social networks,
which added more personal elements and expanded the ability to
identify with other members on a more personal level. Now the sequel is virtual worlds, and yes, as any respectable third sequel should
be, *it's in 3-D!*

And like a child strapping on his first set of blue- and red-lensed
cardboard glasses, there is great anticipation of what can be accomplished in this next iteration of social networks.

STALKING THE PINK-HAIRED AVATAR

By now, we're pretty sure you're getting the message: marketing in the new Internet age is all about the power to engage your consumer. Virtual worlds can make engagement and interaction between marketers and consumers create a strong bond. The largest and most talked about virtual world is Second Life, created and operated by LindenLabs, with about 300,000 to 500,000 unique users. Many audience figures reported in the press are much higher, but the 700,000 to 800,000 "residents" typically reported don't accurately reflect that many users have multiple identities "in world." Even though these numbers aren't as substantial as mammoth social networks like Facebook and MySpace, who boast tens of millions, these early adopters in virtual worlds represent "influentials" who could be important to your brand.

Already, Toyota, Nissan, Coca-Cola, IBM, Cosmopolitan, Microsoft, Adidas, Major League Baseball, and countless others have dipped their virtual toe in these 3-D worlds. MTV and Disney have created their own.

Residents are driving around in virtual cars, shopping at virtual stores, and taking university classes. Do you see what's happening here? They're actively engaging with the brands. American Apparel sells clothing "in world" and has links to their "real-world" online store for anyone interested in trading the blue light of their computer screen for sunlight. As exciting as this may seem, getting a piece of this action has been a disappointing exercise. Many residents came to virtual worlds to get away from banners, so the strategy here is about constructing an environment where your customers can engage with your brand in this cyber dimension as you wish they would in the real world.

So if you're already engaging your consumers in all manner of other Web 2.0 tools like search engines, social networks, widgets, viral videos and blogs, why bother with this up and comer? If you asked this question of those driving the virtual world bus, they'd tell you that the very nature of virtual worlds delivers much deeper—and more measurable—engagement.

Figure 11-1 Harlequin romance readers attend a costume ball on Second Life.

Should you decide to experiment with virtual worlds, you don't need to choose just one. Different worlds have different demographics, goals, rules and ideals. You need to cater your initiative in each environment to be sensitive to the virtual community you're trying to engage. Coca-Cola has most recently created CC Metro in the world There.com after experimenting for several years with its own virtual world Coke Studios at MyCoke.com. Pontiac, Toyota and Nissan and others have virtual dealerships selling fully customizable virtual cars on Second Life (and yes, the residents pay real money at a little over a buck a piece for their fantasy vehicles).

Investigate the membership of these virtual societies and then market to the appropriate worlds. Club Penguin (Disney), NeoPets, Nicktropolis (MTV) and Webkinz are for children. This last is a successful digital migration of the earlier craze for Beanie Babies, from toymaker Ganz. There.com and Second Life, both mentioned above, and Kaneva focus on socialization. MMOGs and Game Domain International (recently acquired by Virgin) are massive multiplayer online game worlds for gamers. Each of these would require a different approach.

Once you've decided where, you really need to think about how deeply you want to engage. You can sell virtual merchandise, have your own area within the world, or create a product they can use in the world like a car. As Michael Wilson, CEO of Makena Technologies, creator of There.com and the technology platform for MTV's franchise-related worlds, points out, "This is the point where the virtual world operator needs to step in to help agencies and brands understand the dynamics of the world to ensure a successful campaign."

If done well, with truly creative implementation, engagement can be significant. "On average, our members spend about 10 minutes interacting with a brand in the world, compared to an average of 12.16 seconds interacting with traditional online advertising. That's a 6,000 percent improvement, which is even more amazing since it's based on actual data," says Wilson.

Whatever you do, don't simply put up a virtual billboard along some virtual highway. Joshua Porter of Bokardo.com, a social web design firm, in his blog post "Why Social Ads Don't Work" (bokardo.com/archives/why-social-ads-dont-work/), posits that people don't click on ads in social networks because they're not there looking for anything. They're there to network and hang out:

> When people go to Google, they're actively looking for something. That something isn't on Google. They are performing a search activity. Thus their task will be to click on a link that seems to promise what it is they're looking for. It may be the organic results, or it may be an ad that seems close to what they want. When people are on MySpace, the activity they're doing isn't search. It's something akin to "hanging out" or "networking". Their task is almost the opposite of search. They are already on the site they want to be on. They don't need to click on links to take them where they want to go.

The playfulness of virtual communities takes a more serious turn when applied to business-to-business communications. Not surprisingly, high-tech companies such as Cisco Systems have most successfully used Second Life and promote it as a vehicle for technical collaborations and customer forums. In June 2008, Cisco CEO John

Chambers addressed a small crowd for a live Q & A session (archived at http://blogs.cisco.com/virtualworlds/comments/thanks_for_the_virtual_cisco_live_memories/). Architectural firms, well accustomed to 3-D renderings, have also been early adopters of Second Life.

ADVERGAMING

Much like virtual worlds, advergaming provides the opportunity for you to achieve deep engagement with your consumers. For certain industries, reaching out to business customers with advergaming may not be a stretch, if you're already providing their bosses with courtside tickets to a basketball game or a few rounds of golf. Why not provide rank-and-file employees with a safe-for-work online diversion while they're stuck in front of their desktop computers?

Advergaming most commonly refers to promoting your brand through online games and computer console games—although some include online contests and promotions in the category. A successful advergaming strategy will enable you to engage, entertain and interact with your consumers through the web, and as soon as the United States catches up with the rest of the world, through mobile phones.

Figure 11-2 Virtual Pamplona shows Unilever is bullish on advergaming

An easy entry into this medium is to purchase online advertising on cutting-edge gaming communities such as Kongregate.com, which displays ads on its chat pages and shares ad revenues with game developers, and Zynga.com, a casual gaming site that often has as many as 6 million poker players participating at the same time. Meez Games (Meez.com) specializes in games that run on mobile phone platforms and can be spread around as widgets. Agencies specializing in game ad insertions include Mochi (mochiads.com), which accepts banners in languages other than English and does not include "adult content" games on its network.

Advergaming strategy can be divided into three categories:

1. You provide interactive games on your site, promote them and wait for your customers to come to the party. The hope is that through positive game play experience your brand will be elevated in their minds and you will achieve more product awareness. These games can feature your product within them for heightened exposure.

2. The second approach is usually more contextual, with the subject matter and plot line more directly relating to your product or service. Unilever in the UK created Extreme Pamplona, an animated "run with the bulls" game that matched the macho for its men's deodorant product Sure™ in European and U.S. markets. If you repair air conditioners, an air conditioner repairman might be a protagonist that uses Freon bombs to foil an evil thermal beast. The U.S. Army uses games like this to entice visitors to consider enlisting. The hope is that if you're interested in the subject matter, you may want to investigate further. Don't be afraid to think bigger. Remember, your goal here is to engage with your consumer. If the demographic you cultivate has common interests or hot buttons, use online games to appeal to those interests and draw them in to your brand—much like Whirlpool does with its American Family podcasts. Kongregate.com and Flashgamelicense.com are

two facilitators that match developers with advertisers to create product-specific games designed to appear on gaming sites or as widgets within social networks.

3. The third category is basically product placement. The game action could be framed by your brand logo, or there could be placement within the game itself. If it's a baseball game, your placement could be a logo on an infield wall, just like a customer would expect to see at a real game. Many companies are working directly with video game developers like Electronic Arts and are purchasing real estate within the game. The game developers like this because it offsets the costs of producing the game and allows them to offer the game to consumers at a better price. Be aware, especially for console games, that static in-game ads are not real time and must be developed months in advance to the game's actual launch. Additionally, these ads cannot change once they are hard-coded into the game. Dynamic in-game ads can be very expensive, depending on the depth of your campaign, but refreshing ads—changing them regularly—can make a stronger impression over time.

When consumers are involved in a game, they are not multitasking, they are actively engaged. Any product message or image woven into the context of the game is much more likely to be retained—and acted upon. Further, consumers spend more time with a game than with other forms of online media. Research shows that on average, customers spend 30 minutes per session interacting with your brand through advergaming. Finally, if your ad is hard-coded into the game, players get a brand impression over and over, every time they play the game.

If a game is exciting, or has multiplayer capability, where the consumer can compete with other netizens, it can go viral. An engaged consumer loves to tell others about a good experience, and can invite others to participate with your brand for you. As stated previously, provide the tools in your advergame to make it easy for your consumers to share with their friends.

Consumers are more likely to click through to an online game than a basic product announcement banner. When they play the game, they become much more likely to share personal data, and ask you to let them know about updates and new features. They opt in and ask you to interact with them. This is the holy grail of online marketing, and advergaming is one of the best vehicles for eliciting this level of interaction.

Within a game, if a consumer becomes interested in a product, he or she can click through to it and investigate further. This of course is measurable, so you can determine interest levels with a product, or new product launch.

Finally, you may hold the misconception that all online gamers are teenage boys. As more games come online, of different genres, there are games that appeal to all segments. The fastest growing segment currently is women older than 26 years of age. Your challenge is to understand what kinds of games appeal to your customer base, and create the games they'll want to come play on your site, and invite their friends to play.

MOBISODES AND WEBISODES

On November 11, 2004, *USA Today* announced the arrival of the mobisode with the headline: "Fox to provide TV series for mobile phones." Twentieth Century Fox, grand dame of the silver screen, then revolutionary on the television screen, was moving to the tiny screen with short episodes of the hit TV series *24* and was partnering with Vodafone to deliver the content around the world. This came to the United States several months later with Verizon.

Television producers realize they're in the content business, not the broadcast television business. Producers at NBC began offering some of the first webisodes with new content and extra plot twists for the show *The Office* in 2006. Trial and error found that consumers weren't prone to download entire 30-minute shows. They were more interested in the YouTube variety shorts, so 2-minute compressed mini episodes ("minisodes") were produced. As these gained in popularity, advertisers weren't far behind with product placement and prequel ads.

Further, when advertisers find shows that resonate with their customer base, they are engaging the consumer by partnering with the network to sponsor webisodes, minisodes with extra plotline or character development that are distributed on the web, and mobisodes, mini blocks of content that are made to be viewed and shared on mobile phones.

Mastercard's product placement in the Fox television show *Bones* extends beyond a character swiping their Mastercard on the show to prominent placement in the show's mobile extension, "Bones: Skeleton Crew." The marketers at Mastercard realize that television is the medium to blanket the masses with ads, but when television combines with the web and with mobile content, brands can get more personal with their consumers.

When Toyota launched the Yaris, they found that the viewership of the Fox show *Prison Break* matched their target market almost identically. So beyond commercials, Toyota serves up short 10-second spots that appear before 2-minute mobisodes of the show. Additionally, they created interactive ad banners featuring cartoon-like dueling Yaris cars.

Moving beyond PG programming is a risk. One interesting side effect of such efforts that you will need to consider is that your company may become the target of well-orchestrated mass email attacks generated by bloggers or third-party websites opposed to your sponsoring of programming that they view as immoral, or condoning immoral acts.

With the Toyota example cited above, Bruce Ertmann, director of consumer-generated media at Toyota Motor Sales USA, takes ownership of such complaints. *Prison Break*, after all, wasn't a prime time tea party. Rather than ignore or dismiss the email attacks as radical, he said, "We've devised an email response system that allows us to reply to each of the complaints—literally thousands and thousands of emails." His group develops the content for the response, which strives to be more sympathetic to the complainers, and points out to the writer the things that Toyota is doing to assure them that the company is not an evil corporate entity.

Even responding to complaints is an opportunity to engage with the consumer. Some, of course, may object to the very idea of advertisements on a video clip viewed over a cell phone. An interesting study out last year by Havas agency Media Contacts and comScore found that the most frequent consumers of web video dislike commercials, but this additional feature of the Internet also draws consumers who don't seem to mind. Four groups were segmented, and if they reliably represent the web video audience there may be happy times ahead.

The first, dubbed "On Demanders," skew to the 18–34 demographic, heavy users of the medium (as much as 250 viewings per month), and are nearly 90 percent more likely to pay for a download to avoid commercials. "Sight and Sounders" tend to be over 55, new to the web, and prefer to watch TV—a behavior that may change once over-the-air broadcasting disappears in 2009. "Television Devotees" were an interesting group, largely female, who use web video to catch up on their favorite programs and are more accepting of advertisements. "Content Explorers" watch a wider variety of programs on the web, long and short, from feature films to amateur clips, fall into the 35–54 category and tend to have higher incomes. It is expected this group would also watch commercials for their entertainment value.

LOCATION-BASED ADVERTISING/MOBILE ADVERTISING

When Steve Jobs announced the Apple iPhone, he made it clear that Apple was going after a much bigger pie than the personal computer market. Who could blame him? Recent estimates peg the number of mobile phones worldwide at 2.5 billion, with personal computers coming up a distant second at a billion or so. Sales growth of the mobile phone market continues to outpace the PC, especially in developing markets. Numbers like this make some marketing pundits predict mobile advertising will one day surpass television, radio, newspaper and outdoor.

In January 2007, at the World Economic Forum in Davos, Switzerland, Google CEO Eric Schmidt said of the mobile web, "It's the recreation of the Internet, it's the recreation of the PC story and it is before us—and it is very likely it will happen in the next year." Those are some big claims Mr. Schmidt, so what does Yahoo! have to say? "We view the mobile Internet today as entering an era where the PC-based Internet was in '96 or '97," said Steve Boom, Yahoo!'s senior vice president for broadband and mobile. "It is just on the cusp of taking off."

Listen to the dueling search executives. The handwriting is on the wall, or in this case the web, and the message is in big, bold letters: THE WEB HAS ALREADY GONE MOBILE.

Mobile Marketing refers to the use of wireless media, the mobile phone, as an integrated content delivery and direct response vehicle. To make the move to the mobile web, several pieces are being put in place.

- *Bandwidth:* A bidding war is heating up for frequency, the 700mHz spectrum, being vacated by broadcast TV in 2009. At the table trying to get the bandwidth are Google, Apple, Paul Allen (Microsoft cofounder who already owns parts of the spectrum), AT&T and ClearWire. I know you're thinking, "So what?," but this frequency is more powerful and can travel longer distances than the frequency currently in use by most carriers. If you're trying to deliver rich content to the mobile phone, you need this.

- *Platform:* The iPhone was the first mobile phone with a big screen and a fully functioning web browser, and the iPhone 3G is considered by many as the first truly mobile computing platform. Other manufacturers are quickly adding multimedia capabilities to their phones, and cellular carriers are working to improve their networks. The trump in all of this could be Google's new open mobile platform, Android. The Android software is written to run on cheap handsets, not just flashy, high-end smart phones. It allows for a variety of input methods, including conventional numeric keypads, QWERTY keyboards and touch screens. Since it is an open platform, enthusiastically supported by the Open Handset

Alliance, applications can come from many developers, increasing functionality and therefore adoption. This has the potential to make the mobile web available to anyone.

- *Infrastructure:* Networks are already in place from independent mobile companies and carriers. Companies like AdMob, Millenial Media, Grey Stripe, Enpocket and AvantGo are mobile ad networks. Sprint, AT&T, Verizon, Moderati and Mblox are carrier networks for mobile ads.

- *Content:* Google Mobile, Yahoo! Go, eBay, CBS Sports, ESPN, WeatherBug and romance publisher Harlequin Enterprises are just a few of the content players who already have staked their territory. Jupiter Research indicates that 40 percent of websites launched a mobile version by the end of 2007, with 22 percent more saying they had plans to launch mobile sites in 2008.

- *Access:* More than 75 percent of mobile phone owners in the United States have access to the Internet through their phones. With the new platforms and networks mentioned above, that number will only grow.

ADS ON WIRELESS APPLICATION PROTOCOL (WAP)

Most advertising to mobile phones today is done with text messaging. But there are, in fact, a number of mobile media formats.

- *Mobile Internet Advertising:* Wireless Application Protocol (WAP) enables website developers to code sites in such a way that they can easily be viewed on mobile phones. When creating content for mobile phones, put yourself in a billboard state of mind. Not in terms of big graphics, but in terms of little messages. You need to be able to deliver your message at a glance. The message is more important than the wrapping.

- *Video:* Streaming/Pre-roll delivers a short video that autoplays (with sound) before video content listed on a site. This is often used by advertisers to be placed in front of webisodes or mobisodes.

- *Short Message Service:* Allows text messages to be sent and received. This is the current state of the union for mobile phone advertising.

- *Multimedia Message Service:* Allows graphics, video clips, and sound files to be sent and received over wireless networks using the WAP protocol. As a marketer, you may use this to deliver ring tones, music promotions or mobisodes that your market enjoys.

- *Downloadable applications:* Java/Brew is an example of a platform for building applications that can be downloaded to a mobile phone or PDA. Apple opened the iPhone platform with the iPhone SDK (software developers kit), and more than 500 independently created applications were launched in June 2008 to accommodate the 3G version. Google's Android, mentioned above, is another wellspring of new applications open to any developer. As penetration of open platforms increases, you have the opportunity to layer applications specific to your brand on top of them. This is taking the widget concept and dropping it into the mobile market.

MOBILE VIDEO SEARCH AS LOCAL SEARCH

When thinking about mobile advertising, it's best to consider context and relevance. If customers are accessing the web from their mobile phone, they are most likely looking for something specific. Maps or directions, restaurant recommendations, airline schedules, news and weather are just a few of the possible reasons they're online. Do the research and find out what are the most commonly accessed categories of sites from a mobile phone, and make your marketing relevant to the data delivered from these sites, and therefore relevant to the potential customer. Yahoo! Go for Mobile 2.0 offers free ad-supported services tailored to match a user's settings, like ZIP code and stock preferences. Go for Mobile is equipped with "oneSearch," which interpret a user's intent and delivers results accordingly. When a user searches for a sports team, the service will make a bet that the user is interested in the latest scores, a team profile and news related to the team, and return those first. Yahoo! has signed agreements with handset makers to preload or distribute the software and is also encouraging users to download the software directly onto their devices.

UK-based IMS Research projected a significant increase in the number of GPS-enabled handsets shipped in 2008, coupled with an increase in AGPS network rollouts worldwide. Its report, "GPS in Cellular," provides forecasts for various cellular technologies. GPS unit revenues are forecast to have a compound annual growth rate of just under 40 percent over the next four years. Those who use the GPS-enabled phones are revealing some interesting statistic, according to IMS:

- A strong majority (60 percent) report that, in the weeks preceding the interview, they had used a geographic website (e.g., MapQuest, Google Maps). This is twice the percentage (30 percent) that report using traditional paper maps.
- 64 percent reported that they were "very satisfied" with the services.
- 72 percent of those who used them for information about restaurants, gas stations or stores similarly reported that they were "very satisfied."

The national poll also found that, in contrast with the usual patterns of adoptions of new technologies, the purchase and use of GPS-enabled devices is not confined to the segment of the population in which "early adopters" are generally concentrated—that is, the young, highly educated or affluent. Today's GPS-enabled devices are being adopted by anyone using maps or other forms of digital mapped data, including the middle-aged and elderly.

As more and more mobile phones are GPS-enabled, or, like the iPhone, able to triangulate location from cellular phone tower locations, carriers will know where their customers are, and will be able to help you with contextual advertising. If you have retail locations in proximity to the customer, send them a coupon or a special discount. If customers frequent certain locations like the beach, or work in the financial district, do the data mining and find out how your offerings may be relevant to beach goers or investment bankers, and serve up an offer based on that information. Yes. This is all very big brother-ish, but it is coming and everyone is hoping that privacy will be respected while still opening the door for marketing opportunities.

WHERE DO YOU GO FROM HERE?

ARE YOU READY to engage your customers with all the tools Web 2.0 can offer?

To get your organization up to speed, here is a handy checklist—a scorecard, in fact—that you can use to gauge where you are competitively, and where you need to be.

We suggest you use the scorecard that follows before you begin creating or rebuilding your brand on the web, and then again, periodically, as you progress.

We wish you luck and success in your ventures and adventures, and invite you to check out the website created for this book, www.digital-engagement.com, for updates and additional insights about today's web media.

—Bob and Leland

DIGITAL ENGAGEMENT SCORECARD

Score your company from 1 to 5; any score below 3 is untapped potential; any score below 2 is an area that should be addressed for serious improvement.

WEB BASICS
How well does your web initiative include the following?
_____ Brand Building
_____ Lead Generation
_____ Online Sales
_____ Customer Support
_____ Market Research
_____ Word of Web
_____ Customer Services
_____ Web Content Publishing
_____ Is your site instrumented for measurement?
_____ Does the organization calculate a useful CPW (cost per whatever) and lifetime customer value?
_____ Are you successfully exploiting the Affiliate channel?

DOMAINS & BRAND PROTECTION
_____ Have you protected all relevant domain names?
_____ Are you vigilantly enforcing your intellectual property rights?
_____ Are you thinking globally?
_____ Are you protecting your brand aggressively on search engines?

SEARCH ENGINE MARKETING
_____ Do you think you are doing enough for effective SEO?
_____ Are you using more than just Google in your search program?
_____ Are you using local and/or international search?
_____ Are you visible on vertical search within your industry or field?

WORD OF WEB
_____ Do you use blogs, wikis, RSS, podcasts or webinars to reach customers?
_____ Have you identified important influencers in your customer base?
_____ Have you done any recent viral marketing campaigns?
_____ Do you use your press releases and blog postings to boost your SEO?

WEB VIDEO
_____ Are you comfortable with Web Video and using it on your site?
_____ Are you helping your videos go viral?
_____ Are you tracking your videos on file sharing sites?
_____ Are your videos helping your SEO?

PAID MEDIA AND DISPLAY ADVERTISING
_____Are you integrating both Search and Display in your ad buys?
_____Are you optimizing your campaigns?
_____Are you utilizing ad networks efficiently?
_____Are you testing potential offline ads on blogs? On Web Video?

MEASUREMENT & METRICS
_____Do you have good site analytics? How often do you review them?_____
_____Are you using site side data to optimize campaigns?
_____Are you reconciling site data with third-party ad server data?
_____Are you using Quantcast.com or Compete.com or a similar service?

DIGITAL ENGAGEMENT
Are you tracking and optimizing user/customer:
_____Loyalty?
_____Recency?
_____Duration of time spent on site?
_____Interactivity?
_____Have you devised a metric to measure customer engagement?

NEW CHANNELS

_____Have you investigated or used online gaming for customer outreach?
_____Are you personally active in MySpace, Facebook, LinkedIn or similar?
_____Have you played in a virtual world?
_____Do you have an iPhone? Or use any other web-enabled handheld?

A Web Marketing Glossary

301 redirect: A message that the URL has moved permanently. This is commonly used when a URL has a new location and will not be appearing again at the old URL.

404 server code: A "not found" message. The server cannot find the requested URL.

A/B testing: Testing that varies and tests only one element at a time.

above the fold: The part of a Web page that is visible without any scrolling. Derives from a newspaper industry term for newspapers such as the *New York Times*.

ad network: A collection of online advertising inventory sold by a common sales force. Usually offer run-of-category and run-of-network buys.

affiliate marketing: A model of revenue sharing that allows merchants to expand their sales efforts by enlisting other websites in the sales effort. Merchants pay affiliates a referral fee when sales are made to customers referred by the affiliate.

algorithm: A set of rules that a search engine uses to rank the listings contained within its index, in response to a particular query.

algorithmic results: *See* organic listings.

ALT text: An HTML tag (ALT tag) used to provide images with a text description in the event images are turned off in a web browser. Also known as "alternative text" or "alt attribute."

anchor text: Words used to link to a page, used by search engines to determine a page's relevance.

API (application programming interface): A technology that allows users to request software services over the web. APIs allow data to be exchanged between computer programs.

attribution: Crediting the proper website or search ad with the resulting conversion.

B to B, B2B: Stands for "Business to Business." A business that markets its services or products to other businesses. Also written "B-to-B."

B to C, B2C: Stands for "Business to Consumer." A business that markets its services or products to consumers.

backlinks: All the links pointing to a particular web page. Also known as "inbound links."

banned: When pages are removed from a search engine's index specifically because the search engine has deemed them to be in violation of guidelines.

behavioral targeting: Targeting and serving ads to groups of people who have similarities in how they interact with online media, including topic areas and shopping categories visited.

bid: The maximum amount of money that an advertiser is willing to pay each time a searcher clicks on a paid search engine ad.

bid management software: Software that automatically manages prices paid for keywords in paid search campaigns.

blacklist: A list of websites that are considered off limits or dangerous, usually because of spamming or inappropriate SEO techniques. In paid web media, a blacklist may refer to a list of competing advertisers restricted from appearing on the same page with a preferred client's ads.

blog: A frequently updated online journal usually intended for public viewing, the shortened form of "web log."

bot: *See* crawler.

brand lift: A measurable increase in consumer recall for a specific, branded company, product or service.

buying funnel: Refers to the multistep process of a consumer's path to purchase. Also known as a "sales funnel," "buying cycle," "buyer decision cycle" or "sales cycle."

buzz marketing: Creating excitement online, leading to purchase. *See also* word of web.

click fraud: Clicks on a PPC (pay per click) ad that are fraudulent. Click fraud may be the result of a malicious competitor or of fraud committed to unfairly earn affiliate commissions.

click-through rate (CTR): The percentage of those clicking on a link out of the total number who are exposed to the link.

content network: Contextual Search networks serve paid search ads triggered by keywords related to the (non search) page content viewed by a user. Also called "contextual network."

contextual advertising: Advertising that is automatically served or placed on a web page based on the page's content, keywords and phrases.

conversion: The desired result of a click-through: an actual sale, sales lead, newsletter signup or other positive action by the user.

conversion rate: The ratio between visitors to a website and actions considered to be a "conversion," such as a sale, email entry, guest registration or request to receive more information.

cost per click (CPC): Where an advertiser pays an agreed amount for each click someone makes on a link leading to their website.

CPA (cost per acquisition, cost per action): The total cost of an ad campaign divided by the number of conversions.

CPM (cost per thousand, cost per impression): Ad impressions are usually sold in blocks of 1,000. Used in print, broadcasting and direct marketing, as well as in online banner ad sales, where the term describes cost per web page impression, a metric that is sometimes (rarely) referred to as CPI.

crawler: A search engine's crawler automatically compiles links to web pages and stores them in the search engine's index. Also called a "spider," "robot" or "bot."

CTR: *See* click-through rate.

dayparting: Specifying different times of day, or day of week, for ad display

delisting: When pages are removed from a search engines index. *See also* banned.

demographic targeting: Demographic targeting allows the advertiser to specify where ads will be shown based on the user's demographic characteristics.

directory: A type of search engine in which listings are gathered and edited by humans rather than by crawlers or bots.

DKI (dynamic keyword insertion): The insertion of the same keywords a searcher included in his or her search request in the returned ad title or description.

doorway page: A web page created expressly for ranking well in search engines. Also known as "jump page" or "gateway page."

dynamic keyword insertion: *See* DKI.

engagement: A soft metric that tries to measure the level of interactivity and loyalty to a product or brand.

freemium: A business model offering free and paid premium content on the same website.

frequency capping: Restricting the amount of times a specific visitor is shown a particular web advertisement.

geo-targeting: Geo-targeting allows the advertiser to specify where ads will be shown based on the user's geographic location.

GRP (gross rating points): The sum of ratings achieved by a specific media vehicle.

home page takeover: Securing all the available advertising space on a publisher's home page.

html (hypertext markup language): The coding language used to describe web formatting and display.

http (hypertext transfer protocol): The coding language that gives directions on the web, and allows a computer user to move from one server location to another.

https (hypertext transfer protocol secure): This is a variant of http that gives directions for movement to, from and within secure sites, used for password-protected web pages and ecommerce. The "s" stands for "secure socket layer."

impression: A single view or display of an ad.

inbound links: *See* backlinks.

index: The search engine's collection of information and links that have been categorized.

IP (Internet protocol) address: A trackable address for any computer, used to localize results.

jump page: *See* doorway page.

keyword: A specific word or combination of words that a searcher might type into a search field.

landing page: The web page that a visitor reaches after clicking a link or an ad.

lead generation: Using a website to generate leads for products or services offered by another company.

lifetime value: The value of a customer based on the estimated or actual number of purchases made over a substantial period of time.

linkbait: Content on a website that attracts other sites to link to it.

link popularity: A measure of how "popular" a page is based on the number of backlinks to it. ALEXA (www.alexa.com) is one site that measures link popularity.

link text: The text contained within a link.

listings: The information that appears on a search engine's results page in response to a search.

log file: Information stored on a server detailing all traffic to and within a website.

long tail: Keyword phrases with multiple words that are highly specific and draw lower traffic than shorter, more competitive keyword phrases, but that often yield a high rate of conversion. Also used to describe the long-term sales performance of older products.

meme: In Internet terms, a catchphrase, coined word or concept that spreads quickly through the web by being passed around through RSS or email.

meta search engine: A search engine that obtains listings from two or more other search engines.

meta tags: Data placed in web page source code that are not intended for users to see but that aid spiders and search engines in categorizing the page.

multivariate testing: Testing that varies and tests more than one or two campaign elements at a time to determine the best performing combinations, unlike A/B testing, which changes only one element at a time.

organic listings: Search engine results that are not sold but are generated by the search engine based on relevancy to the keywords searched for.

outbound links: Links on a particular web page leading to other web pages.

PageRank: PageRank™ is the Google technology for ranking organic search results. Named for Google founder Larry Page.

paid inclusion: A now little-used program in which pages are guaranteed to be included in a search engine's index in exchange for payment.

paid listings: Ads that appear on a search engine results page because of advertiser payment.

pay per click (PPC): *See* cost per click.

podcast: A podcast is an audio media file that is distributed over the Internet using syndication feeds, for playback on portable media players (MP3 players, etc.) and personal computers.

pop-up: An advertisement, usually with an outbound link, that appears in a new browser window, allowing the user to explore the new link without abandoning the current web page.

position: *See* rank.

PPC (pay per click): *See* cost per click.

Quality Score: A number assigned by Google that, together with bid level, determines an ad's rank. Factors contributing to the Quality Score include an ad's historical CTR, keyword relevance, and landing page relevance. Yahoo! refers to the Quality Score as a Quality Index.

query: A request made of a search engine for results for a specific keyword or keyword phrase. Also called "search terms."

rank: How close to the top a particular web page or website is listed in search engine results pages. Also called "position."

reach and frequency: Reach is how many households are exposed to an advertising message, and frequency is how often each household will be exposed to the message. The two numbers multiplied together indicate the total potential audience exposure in a given market.

reciprocal link: A link exchange between two sites.

results page: The page that appears in response to a users search engine query. Also called a "SERP" (search engine results page).

rich media: Web media with embedded motion or interactivity.

robot: *See* crawler.

robots.txt: A file used to keep web pages from being indexed by search engines.

ROI (return on investment): The amount of money invested in advertising compared to the amount of money received.

RSS (rich site summary *or* real simple syndication): A format that uses XML for distributing and sharing information on the web.

search engine marketing (SEM): Generally used to refer to marketing that uses paid search strategies.

search engine optimization (SEO): The practice of enhancing the ranking of a website so that it ranks highly in search engines. Activities include "on page" factors such as metatags and relevancy, and "off page factors" such as inbound links.

search terms: *See* query.

SEM: *See* search engine marketing.

SEMPO (Search Engine Marketing Professional Organization): A nonprofit organization formed to increase the awareness of and educate people on the value of search engine marketing.

SEO: *See* search engine optimization.

SERP: *See* results page.

share of voice: A brand's advertising weight, expressed as a percentage of a defined total market or market segment in a given time period.

social marketing: Utilizing social networks or social media such as Facebook and MySpace, online forums and wikis to spread a marketing message.

social media: Sites where users actively participate and communicate with one another.

spam: Unsolicited and unwelcome email.

spider: *See* crawler.

splash page: The first page of a promotional web page sequence that presents the visitor with choices for further interaction.

submission: The act of submitting a URL for inclusion into a search engine's index.

tag: A bit of html code added to a web page, widget, image or other digital asset, so that it can be counted more easily in an analytics program. *See also* meta tag.

targeting: Focusing ads and keywords to attract a specific potential customer. Techniques include dayparting, geo-targeting, behavioral targeting and demographic targeting.

third-party ad servers: Companies such as DoubleClick and Atlas, which facilitate serving banner ads on websites.

unique visitor: A web surfer tracked by a unique identifier, usually an IP address.

usability: Refers to how easy to use a website is. Factors include ease of navigation, clarity of layout and clarity of text.

viral marketing: A marketing technique that utilizes social networks to spread a marketing message or to build brand awareness, often by encouraging voluntary sharing of branded content.

viral video: Web video content that gains widespread popularity through the process of being shared on the Internet, primarily via video sharing sites like YouTube, but also via email and blogs.

web video: Animated or live-action films, typically short subjects, used for entertainment or marketing outreach.

webisode: A video program specifically or originally produced for display on computers.

widget: A computer application that is portable and can be passed around through RSS, email or simple cut-and-paste of code.

wiki: A web publishing format that allows multiple people to contribute knowledge on a particular topic.

XML (extensible markup language): A coding language that can be customized for web applications, it has sets of specific directions common to web coding.

XML feed: A mechanism in which a search engine is "fed" information about pages via XML, rather than gathering that information through crawling actual pages.

ADDITIONAL GLOSSARIES ON THE WEB

Advertising Glossary: www.advertisingglossary.net

Marketing Terms: www.marketingterms.com/dictionary/a/

MiMi.hu (a glossary of advertising and marketing terms): en.mimi.hu/marketingweb/index_marketingweb.html

Search Engine Dictionary: searchenginedictionary.com

Web Trends Glossary: www.webtrends.com/Resources/WebAnalyticsGlossary.aspx

Webopedia: www.webopedia.com

INDEX